How to Grow
Marijuana

SEEDS &
SEEDLINGS

GERMINATING

WATERING

HYDROPONICS

OUTDOOR
GROWING

INDOOR
GROWING

PEST
CONTROL

HARVESTING
& CURING

THE EASIEST GUIDE TO
GROWING WEED

Murph Wolfson

ADAMS MEDIA

New York   London   Toronto   Sydney   New Delhi

For Erika

Aadamsmedia

Adams Media
An Imprint of Simon & Schuster, Inc.
100 Technology Center Drive
Stoughton, MA 02072

First Adams Media hardcover edition January 2020

ADAMS MEDIA and colophon are trademarks of Simon & Schuster.

For information about special discounts for bulk purchases, please contact Simon & Schuster Special Sales at 1-866-506-1949 or business@simonandschuster.com.

The Simon & Schuster Speakers Bureau can bring authors to your live event. For more information or to book an event contact the Simon & Schuster Speakers Bureau at 1-866-248-3049 or visit our website at www.simonspeakers.com.

Interior design by Priscilla Yuen
Interior images by Eric Andrews

Manufactured in the United States of America

5 2021

Library of Congress Cataloging-in-Publication Data
Names: Wolfson, Murph, author.
Title: How to grow marijuana / Murph Wolfson.
Description: Avon, Massachusetts: Adams Media, 2020.
Includes index.
Identifiers: LCCN 2019038280 | ISBN 9781507212585 (hc) | ISBN 9781507212592 (ebook)
Subjects: LCSH: Cannabis. | Marijuana.
Classification: LCC SB295.C35 W65 2020 | DDC 633.7/9--dc23
LC record available at https://lccn.loc.gov/2019038280

ISBN 978-1-5072-1258-5
ISBN 978-1-5072-1259-2 (ebook)

Acknowledgments

I've been writing this book in my head since I was a teenager and planted my first seed, thus launching a lifelong relationship with the marijuana plant. Like so many kids getting into growing back then, I've never met most of the people I would want to thank for their help on this topic—authors and editors of magazines and books I hid under the couch, admins of websites devoted to growing (especially the original version of Overgrow.com), and individuals who were happy to share their knowledge with me from the anonymous safety of message boards and forums. So this thank you is really for the community of people who have never wavered in their drive to grow better marijuana.

For the privilege of writing the book itself, I have to thank two editors at Adams Media: Jacqueline Musser and especially Rebecca Tarr Thomas, along with the keen eye of Sarah Doughty. Working with you has been a wonderful experience, and I'm thrilled to have the opportunity to share this passion. Thanks also to the artists and designers who created such a beautiful cover and illustrations.

And finally, thank you to the millions of people who have tirelessly advocated and voted to help change the laws governing marijuana use and research. It's because of you that we are finally able to treat marijuana with the respect it's earned as one of humankind's most vital and important crops.

Contents

Contents

CHAPTER 6

Stages of Marijuana Growth:

CHAPTER 7

Stages of Marijuana Growth:

Introduction

Looking to grow your own marijuana, but not sure where to start? Maybe past experiences with a less-than-green thumb have you wondering whether you are even capable. Or you assume that it's too time-consuming for one person to manage without working around the clock. The truth is, even if you've never successfully grown so much as a houseplant, you can grow good marijuana. All it takes is a little patience and some basic information.

How to Grow Marijuana takes you through the process of growing your own marijuana in an accessible, step-by-step way. You'll also find a full chapter on the fundamentals of the plant. Understanding the marijuana plant is crucial to success in growing your own, and this chapter provides everything you need to know in an easy-to-follow format that won't have you scratching your head and wondering, "Okay, but what *is* a cannabinoid?"

You'll discover answers to all of your questions—not only about the growing process, but also about marijuana itself—including:

- "What is a strain?"

- "What's the difference between marijuana and hemp?"

- "What kind of equipment will I need for growing recreational marijuana?"

- "When should I harvest it?"

- "How do I prepare my harvest for recreational use?"

And if you *are* interested in digging deeper, we've included pro tips and additional information throughout the book that introduce you to more advanced concepts and techniques that can supercharge your grow.

Every grower is a little bit different, with a unique environment and approach to growing marijuana, and you'll quickly find that you, too, can develop your own signature plants, with the flavor profile, potency, and effect you're looking for. So, let's get started.

CHAPTER 1

What Is Marijuana?

So, you're interested in growing marijuana, but all of the vocabulary you've heard thrown around—what is a "strain," exactly?—has you feeling a bit intimidated and out of your element. And that's okay! Between the "light cycles," "trichomes," and even the various terms for the plant itself, it can seem like a lot to wrap your head around. You may even wonder whether there is a certification or six-week class you are supposed to take before being "qualified" to buy, much less *grow*, marijuana. The truth, however, is that all you really need to understand marijuana is a little background information, a simple guide to the terminology, and a few tips on identifying different marijuana plants.

And this chapter is here to help! Think of it as your crash course on marijuana. First, you'll go back in time to understand a little more of the history of the plant itself and how it came to be one of humankind's most beloved crops. Next, you'll journey through the life cycle of marijuana, from sprouting to harvesting the plant. Finally, you'll learn just what a "strain" is—and the differences between specific marijuana plants. Ready to impress others with your weed expertise? Let's dive in!

MARIJUANA: A BRIEF HISTORY

Marijuana—also known scientifically as "cannabis"—has been a part of the human experience since before recorded history. In fact, it's believed that humans and marijuana evolved together, which makes sense if you consider that the human body has CB1 and CB2 cannabinoid receptors spread throughout almost every major organ system, and that it produces its own cannabinoids, called "endocannabinoids," or chemicals that resemble the active elements of the marijuana plant.

The long history of marijuana makes it somewhat hard to trace its exact roots, but it's thought that the plant is native to central Asia (e.g., Mongolia or the Himalayas). These early marijuana plants were hardier than modern plants and had few of the psychoactive compounds that are valued in marijuana today. However, marijuana is a highly useful plant even if it's not consumed for its psychoactive properties, and it's likely that early populations used it for seed oil, fiber, and even food.

At some point in antiquity, however, people discovered that marijuana had psychoactive compounds. In fact, in 2019, researchers in western China discovered wooden braziers in ancient tombs in the Jirzankal Cemetery that revealed that people were using marijuana in shamanic or religious rituals as early as 2,500 years ago. Testing revealed that these braziers contained the signature chemicals left behind when tetrahydrocannabinol (THC)—the psychoactive chemical in marijuana—is burned.

From there, marijuana seemed to rapidly spread across the rest of the ancient world. In the first millennium B.C.E., the famous Greek historian Herodotus wrote in the *Histories* about the Scythians, an ancient nomadic tribe who used specialized marijuana tents to burn the herb, trapping the smoke inside for the occupants to enjoy. Other accounts from the same era place marijuana in north and east Russia, as well as deeper into western China.

From this early and fertile "weed basket," marijuana steadily moved west along the Silk Road, into modern Afghanistan, Greece and Rome, and finally Europe. Apparently, the ancients knew a good thing when they saw it.

⇢ WHAT IS HEMP?

Although it gets much less press, the US has slowly moved toward legal farming of hemp. This incredibly useful and vigorous plant is one variety of marijuana, specifically *Cannabis sativa*, that has been bred to have negligible quantities of THC, meaning that it has no psychoactive effect. Across the world, hemp has been used for centuries to create clothing, paper, car parts, and other products.

PARTS OF THE MARIJUANA PLANT

All marijuana plants share the same basic biology. In the following sections, you'll discover more about each main component of marijuana.

ROOTS AND STEMS

Roots are responsible for transporting water and nutrients into the plant from the chosen growing medium (soil, a soilless mix, or pure water). The stem provides structure and support to the plant. In general, marijuana grows from a single woody main stem that branches as the plant gets taller and fills out.

LEAVES

The marijuana leaf shape is instantly familiar, with an odd number of serrated leaf blades (typically five to nine) fanning out from a central stem. The shape of the leaves can differ depending on the strain. *C. sativa* leaves tend to be longer and thinner, while *C. indica* leaves are broader and shorter. (See Figure 1.1.) Strains, *C. sativa*, and *C. indica* will all be discussed later in this chapter.

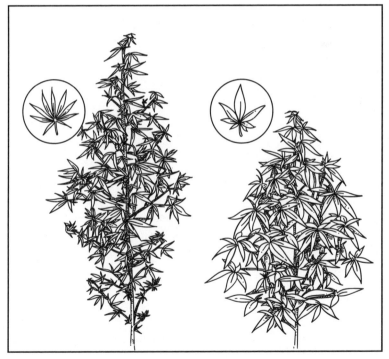

▲ Figure 1.1: *Sativa* versus *Indica*

FLOWERS

Marijuana is known as a "dioecious" plant. This means that male and female flowers are borne on separate, individual plants. For marijuana to breed, a male plant has to be growing close enough to a female plant to pollinate her flowers, which will then begin to produce seeds. In general, marijuana cultivators focus only on female plants and destroy male plants and hermaphrodites before they have a chance to pollinate the females. The reason for this is simple: The flower, or bud, of the female marijuana plant is what we consume, and unpollinated females produce much stronger, more potent buds with more THC-rich resin.

WHAT ARE MARIJUANA HERMAPHRODITES?

Marijuana is a dioecious plant most of the time—but not always. Under certain circumstances, a single plant will contain both male and female flowers. These are known as "hermaphrodites." Hermaphrodites are capable of self-pollinating, which means the plant's buds will always contain seeds. This plant can also pollinate other nearby females. If you find a hermaphrodite in your crop, you should remove it and destroy it as quickly as possible to prevent pollination of your females.

SEEDS

Seeds are produced from pollinated females. Unless you're breeding marijuana, you usually don't want seeds, because it takes extra energy to produce seeds, energy that could be used instead to produce more resin and stronger buds.

WHAT IS SINSEMILLA?

Unpollinated female plants produce marijuana that is known as "sinsemilla," from the Spanish word meaning "without seed." Sinsemilla is produced by keeping your female plants away from any male plants or hermaphrodites so they are never pollinated. As you get better at growing marijuana, you'll learn to keep an early eye out for preflowers—which occur after the plant is sexually mature—so you can quickly identify and remove your male plants, leaving your females free to pour their energy into producing bigger, stronger, and "frostier" buds.

THE LIFE CYCLE OF THE MARIJUANA PLANT

Marijuana is a naturally resilient plant that has been adapted to a wide range of growing conditions. Even under poor conditions, marijuana can thrive, and in certain parts of the world, feral or wild marijuana is common, sometimes to the point of being a nuisance. Even in the US, so-called "ditch weed" can be found growing along roadsides, thanks to birds and animals that spread the seeds (likely from the crop of an enterprising outdoor grower). In some regions, ditch weed is common enough that it's hard to grow true sinsemilla (seedless females) outside, because there is persistent marijuana pollen in the air.

As a grower, you'll still want to become finely attuned to marijuana's life cycle so you can provide the best nutrition at every stage, and learn how to anticipate and cater to its needs. After all, a pampered plant will produce the highest quality marijuana. These stages are covered in greater detail later in the book, but you'll find an overview here. While the time frames given in this section are approximations, they will give you an idea of what to expect. In general, you should be able to take a marijuana plant from seed to harvest in three to four months, depending on the variety:

- **Germination.** The act of sprouting seeds. Germination time depends on the specific seeds, but can happen as quickly as overnight, or take up to three weeks. Under typical circumstances, seeds will germinate in two to ten days.

- **Seedling.** Your marijuana makes the transition from a sprouted seed to a very fragile and tender young plant. During this phase, your plants may need to be supported with thin bamboo stakes. Seedlings always start with a pair of oval, nonserrated leaves called "cotyledon" leaves. These embryonic leaves are designed to provide the plant with a burst of photosynthetic energy so it can transition to the next phase. The seedling phase lasts anywhere from one to three weeks.

- **Vegetative growth.** During this stage, the marijuana plant will put out mature leaves with increasing vigor and speed, and the stem will thicken and become woody and tough. During vegetative growth, think of your plants as teenagers: They are hungry all the time, and need plenty of light and nutrients to achieve optimal growth. If you're growing indoors, you'll want to provide 18 hours of light every day. As the plant matures, it will eventually reach the maximum number of individual blades on each leaf. Some plants can have as many as ten or eleven blades, but typical marijuana plants will have between five and nine blades on each leaf. Vegetative growth typically lasts between one and five months, depending on the strain and your growing conditions.

- **Preflowering.** The preflowering stage occurs just before the plant goes into full flower and usually lasts between one and two weeks. By this stage, the plant is sexually mature and will likely have already produced some preflowers, but their development will accelerate rapidly during preflowering. Preflowers emerge where the stems meet the branches (these areas are known as "nodes")—often between the fourth and sixth nodes from the bottom of the plant. Early on, it can be difficult to see these tiny flowers without a magnifying glass, but as the plant grows and matures, they will become easier to see. Female preflowers develop telltale fuzzy white pistils (the female sex organs), while male preflowers develop little sacs of pollen.

- **Flowering.** During flowing, the marijuana plant will produce mature flowers. In a male plant, the flowers form on drooping branches. In a female plant, the flowers form around the stems, gradually filling out into more recognizable buds. In indoor growing, many growers trim their plants to form a single large bud on top of the plant called a "cola." If a female plant has been pollinated, this is also when seeds will form inside the growing flowers. If it has not been pollinated, the flowers will increase their resin production. Typically, flowering times range from about eight weeks to twelve weeks or more depending on the strain.

- **Harvest.** At harvest time, you'll cut the plants down to trim and manicure the buds, in preparation for drying and curing your marijuana.

⚘ WHAT ARE LIGHT CYCLES?

If you're wondering what causes marijuana to move through the stages of its life cycle, the answer is simple: the light cycle. Whether grown indoors or out, marijuana is sensitive to the photoperiod (the term used to describe the hours of dark and light in a typical 24-hour period). As a rule of thumb, during vegetative growth an indoor plant will need at least 18 hours of light daily, which you supply using grow lights. Outdoors, the light cycle is determined by the season.

PRO TIP: INDOOR LIGHTING

To trigger flowering, indoor growers shift the photoperiod to 12 hours of dark and 12 hours of light.

MARIJUANA SPECIES

Marijuana can be broken down into the following classification:

- Kingdom: Plantae
- Division: Magnoliophyta
- Class: Magnoliopsida
- Order: Rosales
- Family: Cannabaceae
- Genus: *Cannabis* L.
- Species: *C. sativa* L.

Within this scientific hierarchy, *C. sativa* L. is further broken down into three main subspecies:

- *C. sativa*
- *C. indica*
- *C. ruderalis*

You'll learn more about each of these later in this book, but for now just keep in mind that they are distinct from one another in the way they grow, look, smell, and taste, and in the ways they are used in modern marijuana cultivation and breeding. As a grower, you'll focus on *C. indica* and *C. sativa*, as these are the strains people grow to consume. By contrast, *C. ruderalis* is used by breeders to produce strains with highly desired qualities, but it is not grown to consume on its own. Because they are technically the same species, all of these strains can be crossbred (combined), just like wine grapes can be crossed to create new varietals. This allows breeders to create strains that have specific qualities they want, such as a particular effect, certain growing patterns, or even a highly desirable look.

PRO TIP: EXPLORE STRAINS

Walk into any weed dispensary and you'll be greeted with a dizzying array of strains, much like the variety of wines seen in a fine wine shop. These are the product of decades of breeding efforts, as growers have combined the three main strains in various ways to achieve different effects. Medical growers, for example, are often looking for a certain therapeutic effect in their marijuana, while connoisseurs often breed their plants to produce a specific look, taste, smell, or feel. The website www.leafly.com is an excellent resource to read more about different strains and find user reviews. Take some extra time to explore strains, and consider what you might want in your own grow.

UNDERSTANDING CANNABINOIDS

Marijuana is a prized plant thanks to its high concentration of important phytochemicals (the chemical compounds produced by plants), including cannabinoids, terpenes (the aromatic oils that give the plant its distinctive flavor profiles), and phenolic compounds (which include antioxidants and other chemicals studied for their health benefits). The most important of these are the cannabinoids. Similar in structure to the cannabinoids you produce in your body (called "endocannabinoids"), this group of chemicals has pharmaceutical effects and is studied in a wide range of diseases, from seizure disorders to pain management and cancer therapy.

The cannabinoids in marijuana are able to interact with your body thanks to two special receptors, called the "CB1" and "CB2" receptors, found in many of your cells. Generally, CB1 receptors are located in the nervous system, reproductive organs, and connective tissues, while CB2 receptors are found in the immune system. Some tissues, however, have both CB1 and CB2 receptors.

Interestingly, cannabinoid receptors were named after the plant. They were first discovered while researchers were studying how and why marijuana affects people. At the same time, scientists realized that humans produce their own cannabinoids. As a result, we recognize two main classes of cannabinoids:

- **Endocannabinoids.** These are the cannabinoids produced by the human body.

- **Phytocannabinoids.** These are the cannabinoids produced by the marijuana plant.

In all, there are approximately ninety recognized phytocannabi-noids, the most useful being:

- Tetrahydrocannabinol (THC)
- Cannabidiol (CBD)
- Cannabinol (CBN)
- Cannabigerol (CBG)
- Tetrahydrocannabivarin (THCV)
- Cannabichromene (CBC)

The two most important of these are THC and CBD. THC is the cannabinoid that produces the "high" effect associated with marijuana consumption. CBD, meanwhile, has wide-ranging medi-cal uses, including easing anxiety and helping you both fall and stay asleep. In 2018, the US Food and Drug Administration approved the first CBD-based pharmaceutical drug. The drug in question helps to prevent seizures in two rare and serious forms of epilepsy.

FIVE TIPS TO REMEMBER

Now that you have a basic understanding of the marijuana plant, it's time to start planning your grow! The rest of this book is devoted to the details of growing excellent marijuana, either indoors or out; but to end this first chapter, here are five tips that will help you along the way:

1 **Start with a plan.** In many ways, the success of your grow is made before you germinate your first seed. Before you spend money on seeds and equipment, it's a good idea to read through this whole book so you can make informed decisions.

2 **Keep notes.** Good growers keep track of their growth. This means noting everything that affects your plants, from the germination rate, to your fertilizer schedule and any pest problems, to your flowering times and harvest. As you continue to improve, these notes will form the foundation of your knowledge and help you become a better marijuana gardener.

3 **Don't be afraid to ask for help.** There are plenty of online forums and social media sites where growers exchange tips and advice, not to mention share in the camaraderie of growing marijuana.

4 **Be safe and careful.** This is related to good planning, but make sure your growing area is secure, and there are no fire or other safety hazards.

5 **Keep learning!** There is always more to learn, even for experienced growers, and there are new strains coming out all the time. This might be some of the most rewarding research you'll ever do.

So, with that said, it's time to get down to business and start the journey to growing your own marijuana!

CHAPTER 2

Seeds and Seedlings

Now that you understand the basics of the marijuana plant, you are ready to start planning your grow. Before you actually plant any seeds, you have two main decisions to make. The first is whether you will grow your plants indoors or outdoors. The second is what strain of marijuana you want to grow. What you decide will affect what seeds you buy, and how you care for those seeds so that they can flourish.

In this chapter, you'll first explore each growing and strain option so you can set yourself up for success when it comes to growing your marijuana plants. Then, you'll learn how to go about purchasing seeds based on your choices. Following this, you'll find a crash course in germinating your seeds and caring for the resulting seedlings. So let's get started!

TAKING A SIDE: INDOOR VERSUS OUTDOOR MARIJUANA GARDENING

Today's marijuana growers can be divided into two camps: those who swear that the outdoors is the best possible place to grow superior marijuana, and those who insist upon the total environmental control of an indoor grow to produce the highest quality marijuana.

Your choice of an indoor or outdoor grow will also affect your choice of strain (or strains, if you decide to grow more than one variety). Outdoor growers tend to focus on plants with a *sativa* influence, because these plants typically grow larger and need more room. Indoor growers often focus on strains that have more *indica* influence because they are shorter and easier to manage in a small space.

PRO TIP: ALWAYS RECORD YOUR GROWS

No matter how they grow their plants, experienced marijuana growers learn more with each crop, and use this expanding knowledge to adapt their techniques over time. This is why it is so important to keep comprehensive records at every stage of the growing process. By tracking everything you do, and how your plants react to each of these actions, you'll learn what works and what doesn't, so you can improve your grows in the future.

INDOOR VERSUS OUTDOOR: PROS AND CONS

Now that you have some basic information on indoor versus outdoor growing, let's take a deeper look at the pros and cons of each. Before you think about what strain you want to grow, spend some time considering your unique situation and reviewing the positives and negatives outlined in the following chart. Then, make the call: inside or outside.

OUTDOOR GROWING	
PROS	**CONS**
• Natural sunlight • Room for larger plants • Higher yields • Lower costs • Less equipment may be required	• Dependent on climate • Risk of plants being attacked by pests, animals, and disease • More physically challenging • Plants are vulnerable to theft • Possibility of reduced potency
INDOOR GROWING	
PROS	**CONS**
• Excellent control over growing environment • Less risk of plants being stolen • Ability to produce very high-quality marijuana	• More expensive • More equipment required • Dedicated growing space required • Harder to control pest infestations and diseases

⟩ WHAT IS GUERRILLA GROWING?

Before it was possible for many people to grow marijuana on their own property, growers would use either public land or someone else's land. This is called "guerrilla growing" and is common in many places throughout the world. Guerrilla growing can enable experienced growers to produce very large crops. However, guerrilla growing has its downsides, including the risk of thieves stealing your crop. It can also be physically demanding to set up a large guerrilla grow, often involving backpacking heavy equipment such as pumps and piping into remote areas.

CHOOSING YOUR STRAIN

Once you've figured out whether you are growing indoors or outdoors, you can begin to seriously think about what strain you want to grow. As noted previously, indoor growers often focus on *indica*-dominant plants, while outdoor growers primarily choose *sativa*-dominant strains. Whatever you choose, it's a good idea when first starting out to stick with established strains that have settled genetics, as opposed to "landrace" strains that require more expertise to successfully bring to harvest.

⟫ WHAT ARE LANDRACE STRAINS?

Landrace strains are unique strains of marijuana that have evolved in a natural environment and have never been crossed with another strain. These strains tend to be either pure *indica* or pure *sativa*. An example would be the famous Hindu Kush, an *indica* landrace strain native to the Afghanistan mountains. Landrace strains tend to be more difficult to grow, because the plants are evolved to grow in a particular environment and lack some of the hardiness that comes with good breeding. In general, landrace strains are rare, so almost all of the strains you'll see available are actually crosses.

As outlined previously, most marijuana strains are categorized by whether they are *sativa*-dominant or *indica*-dominant. They are often referred to simply as *indica* or *sativa*, even if they have mixed genetics. As you're researching strains, there are a few things to keep in mind with both types. These main traits and differences are outlined here.

Sativa-Dominant Strains
- Are perfect for growing outdoors
- Often grow very large, reaching 10' or taller
- Can yield a pound or more of marijuana from each individual plant
- Provide a head-tripping, energetic high
- Thrive in most climates, from lower-altitude alpine to tropical ecosystems

Examples of *sativa*-dominant strains include Early Pearl, Lemon Skunk, and AK-47.

*Indica-*Dominant Strains
- Are well suited for growing indoors
- Are typically shorter than *sativa*-dominant strains
- Provide a calming, possibly therapeutic high

Examples of *indica*-dominant strains include Blueberry, Bubblicious, White Rhino, and Skunk Kush.

PRO TIP: SPRING FOR HIGH-QUALITY SEEDS

Although many growers have started with simple bag seed (seeds of murky genetics left over in a bag of non-sinsemilla marijuana), it's recommended that you avoid beginning your own grow journey with low-quality seeds. Your marijuana will only be as good as the time, money, and effort you invest—and that means getting the best genetics you can by purchasing high-quality seeds.

There are dozens of strains of *sativa*-dominant and *indica*-dominant marijuana strains on the market, so take the time to check out more information online. Look into what is popular, especially for new growers, and if you know any growers, talk to them about their chosen strains. You will also find additional resources in the back of this book for helping you explore strains.

FINDING SEEDS

Once you've decided on a strain, it's time to purchase your seeds. Here are the main things you'll want to consider when looking for seeds:

1 **People you know.** If you know someone who grows great marijuana, this is one of the best and most secure ways to get your own seeds (or clones!). (See the Cloning section in this chapter for more information on clones.) It guarantees you are getting the genetics you want, and it supports your fellow growers by giving them your business.

2 **Online groups.** If you don't know anyone who grows marijuana, you can meet people online. There are many established *Facebook* groups, *Reddit* forums, and other websites out there where growers congregate to exchange tips, answer questions, and buy seeds and plants. Do some research to find the most trustworthy online sources. This thriving community is willing to help—you just need to ask!

3 **Seed banks.** Seed banks are breeders and sellers of marijuana seeds. If you use a seed bank, make sure it's a reputable one, and do your research before placing any type of order. Look for seed banks with an established online presence that includes a dot-com address, email or phone support, and other indications of a legitimate business. You can often also find seed bank recommendations, grow reports, and reviews online (just be aware that like with other e-tailers, fake reviews are everywhere). It's also a good idea to contact the seed bank ahead of your purchase. Good seed banks can help you decide on a strain, and you can ask questions about their security, shipping, turnaround time, return policy for crushed or damaged

seeds, and more. Also confirm that your chosen seed bank delivers to your shipping location, especially if you use a PO box.

4 **Payment method and shipping details.** Never buy seeds with your credit card. Instead, use money orders, cash, or cryptocurrencies like Bitcoin. And if possible, have seeds shipped to a place that isn't your home, or where you will be growing.

5 **Cost.** Expect to spend a little money; seeds are typically sold in packets of ten or twenty, and you will pay more for good quality. Remember: Good genetics are worth it, so plan this into your grow budget.

GERMINATING SEEDS

When you receive your seeds, be sure to first check them over. Healthy marijuana seeds are firm and slightly ovoid, with a brown and sometimes streaky or mottled appearance. They should not be split, wrinkled, or dried out.

Once you are satisfied with the seeds you've purchased, it's time to germinate them. This is also called "sprouting" and occurs when your seed first begins to grow. Marijuana seeds typically germinate between two and ten days, but some may take longer depending on the temperature and the seeds themselves. Germinating will almost always be done indoors, regardless of whether you choose to grow your plants indoors or out.

Germinating marijuana seeds is not difficult, and there a few ways you can accomplish it. In the sections that follow, you will discover these different modes for germination. Review each one before choosing which one sounds right for your grow.

PRO TIP: START SLOW

When germinating your seeds, it's a good idea to be prepared for some disappointments at first, and to take precautions—especially when you've spent good money and waited weeks to receive your seeds. It's unlikely that even the best seeds will have a 100 percent germination rate, so if you ordered ten seeds, try germinating only five at first, followed by the other five seven to ten days later. You might even consider starting with just three seeds, then germinating a few more, then a few more, etc. And of course, record your germination rates so you can figure out which germination approach works best for you.

In addition to the main germination methods, you can also start seeds directly in small containers, such as 3″ or 4″ peat pots filled with seedling soil. Simply fill the container with soil, water it until moist, and bury one seed in each container. Seeds should be buried to a depth equal to the length of the seed. Once you've planted the seeds, you can move the containers to a growing rack under lights, or put them in a tray with a dome. Keep them warm (between 75°F and 80°F) and moist until the tiny leaves emerge.

EXPANDABLE PEAT PELLETS

These little discs of sphagnum peat, commonly known as "Jiffy pellets," are widely available in home improvement and garden stores. Here's how to use them to germinate your marijuana seeds:

1 Put the discs into a large tray, each disc spaced a few inches apart.

2 Pour room-temperature water over them until they expand.

3 Place one seed in each expanded pellet, burying it up to about the depth of the seed itself.

4 Store the tray in a warm, dark place until the first immature leaves (called "cotyledon" leaves) emerge, making sure to keep the pellets continuously moist, but not soaked. Aim for a temperature between 75°F and 80°F.

You'll know your seeds have germinated successfully and are now entering the seedling stage when the first very small green leaves poke through the soil. During the seedling stage, you can keep your seedlings in the peat pellets.

CHEESECLOTH OR PAPER TOWEL

This is a common and low-tech method to germinate your seeds. A cheesecloth can be purchased at any grocer or home goods store, or you can use paper towels that you likely already have on hand. Just follow these simple steps to germinate your seeds:

1 Soak your seeds in a bowl of fresh, clean, room-temperature water for 3 hours.

2 Transfer seeds to a damp cheesecloth or damp paper towel on a large plate.

3 Scatter the seeds loosely, then cover them with another layer of damp cheesecloth or damp paper towel.

4 Store the plate in a warm, dark place, preferably with the plate propped up at an angle or completely vertical to encourage the taproot (main root) to grow downward. Again, your seeds will germinate more quickly if you can provide a warm temperature between 75°F and 80°F.

5 Spritz the paper towel or cheese cloth with water once each day to keep the seeds moist. In this method, it's easy to let the seeds dry out or rot, so be careful with your watering, and keep a record of each time you water.

6 Check your seeds after three days to see if the tiny white taproots have begun to emerge. This is called "tailing," because the emerging root looks like a little white tail.

Once the taproots have emerged, the seeds will be ready to carefully transplant into their seedling containers. This is not your final growing container: Seedling containers are the first small containers where your plants will start their lives before being transplanted into their final homes for vegetative growth. Refer to the section on seedlings later in this chapter for more information.

ROCKWOOL GERMINATING TRAYS

Rockwool is a fibrous material that has excellent water- and air-conducting properties. The Rockwool used in seed germination is typically sold in 2" cubes. Rockwool germinating trays are very popular among both indoor and indoor growers, as they have a high germination rate and can be easily adapted to container gardening, hydroponic setups, and anything in between.

If you're interested in using Rockwool as your germination method, consider buying a seed starter kit containing Rockwool cubes. These are widely available online and come with the Rockwool cubes, a tray, a dome to retain humidity, and rooting hormones. Just be aware that seeds must be correctly placed in the Rockwool, or else some of the seeds may "heave" out of the medium (get pushed up and out of the medium by their own emerging roots) and die.

When using Rockwool, you should also take appropriate safety precautions. Rockwool produces tiny fibers that can be unsafe to inhale. It's a good idea to wear a respirator or facemask to prevent inhaling any of the fibers.

To use Rockwool to germinate your seeds:

1 Soak the Rockwool cubes in a large tray of room-temperature water for up to 24 hours. This will not only help saturate the Rockwool, but also give you a chance to correct the pH level of the Rockwool. As a growing medium, Rockwool has a pH of about 7.8. This is more alkaline than marijuana prefers (remember that a higher pH is alkaline and a lower pH is acidic). You can adjust the pH by using common products like pH Down from General Hydroponics to get the Rockwool to an ideal range of 5.8 to 6.3 pH.

2 After the Rockwool is soaked, slot one seed into the small opening in each cube, pushing it down far enough that it doesn't push out during germination. The ideal depth is about the length of one seed.

3 Keep the tray covered with the dome (if you purchased a kit), or some kind of plastic, ventilated covering to encourage higher humidity and warmth. Make sure to open the slots on the dome to allow for air exchange. You can also prop the cover up to ensure good airflow.

4 Store the tray in a warm location, but don't expose it to direct sunlight, which can cook the seeds. The ideal temperature is between 75°F and 80°F. A temperature below 70°F will result in slow growth, while a temperature above 90°F will reduce your germination rate.

While you're waiting for your seeds to germinate, it can be tempting to mess with them, checking them often or even, if applicable, trying to gently push the soil aside to see if they've germinated. Resist this urge! Seeds appreciate peace and quiet.

Once the first immature leaves have emerged, you will enter the seedling phase. One of the great advantages of using Rockwool is that you don't have to transplant the tender sprouts like you would with the cheesecloth or paper towel method. With Rockwool, you can simply grow the seedlings in the cubes they sprouted in. Refer to the section in this chapter on seedlings for more information on growing your seedlings.

PRO TIP: SKIP THE EXTRAS

Your marijuana seeds should not need any fertilizer, hormones, or other special solutions or products during the germination stage. In fact, seeds and seedlings are very vulnerable to fertilizer, which can easily damage their tender roots (called "burning") and kill them. When you're just starting out as a grower, it's recommended that you simply use clean water (distilled water is a good choice, as the seed itself has all the nutrients and hormones it needs to start life) and hold off on any type of germinating chemical until you're more experienced. This is true even if you bought a starter kit that came with Rockwool cubes and germinating hormones. The only chemical you might need is pH Down while soaking the Rockwool, but once you've planted the seeds, you'll use regular water.

CARING FOR SEEDLINGS

When your seeds first sprout, they will produce a set of leaves called "cotyledon" leaves. These are embryonic leaves that are designed to kick-start the biological processes of life. Cotyledon leaves do not look like typical marijuana leaves: They are oval with smooth margins. (See Figure 2.1.) You can always tell a seedling that's been grown from a seed rather than cloned because of the cotyledon leaves on the stem. Under normal circumstances, these leaves will fall off after the plant begins putting out mature, serrated leaves.

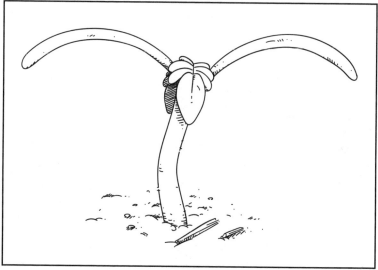

▲ Figure 2.1: Seedling

After your young marijuana seedlings have emerged, you'll need to pay careful attention to them so they thrive. As with the germination stage, the seedling stage will always take place indoors, regardless of whether you choose to grow your plants indoors or outdoors. If you used peat pellets or Rockwool to germinate your seeds, you will continue to grow your seeds in the seedling stage in this germination medium. If you used the cheesecloth or paper towel method, you will need to transplant the seedlings to a new container. An excellent option for seedling containers are fiber pots that are biodegradable and easy to transplant later. You'll also want to start with a gentle growing medium that's designed for seedlings (these are usually labeled for seedlings). Carefully transplant your seedlings to their seedling containers with tweezers. Bury them about ¼" deep in the soil, with the "tail" pointing down.

Seedlings are tender by nature, so it's easy to get excited and overdo it with watering and feeding. As you're caring for your new seedlings, here are some key tips to help ensure your success:

- **Offer adequate lighting.** Provide a minimum of 18 hours of light per day, and up to 24 hours of continuous light (recommended). Most growers use continuous light for seedlings.

- **Choose your lights wisely.** Use either regular fluorescent lights or full-spectrum LED grow lights. LED lights are highly recommended, as they are inexpensive and don't emit a lot of heat. Basic LED grow lights will be adequate for your seedlings.

- **Avoid too much heat.** Position your lights the recommended distance from the tops of the container or seedlings, often within a few inches of the top leaves. In general, your lights will be just a few inches above the plants, to give them the most light possible. Test with your hand to make sure you're not exposing your seedlings to excessive heat.

- **Watch the humidity.** Keep seedlings in an environment of around 80°F, with high humidity. If humidity is low, leave the grow dome on longer, or mist the seedlings daily.

- **Practice good watering.** Keep the growing medium continuously moist, but never waterlogged, and don't let it dry out (see the Prevent "Damping Off" sidebar in this chapter).

- **Give support if needed.** As your seedlings grow, it may be necessary to prop them up with thin bamboo stakes to prevent them from falling over. It's common to use two or even three stakes per seedling to ensure they are fully supported. Be gentle when inserting the stakes, to avoid damaging the seedlings.

- **Be cautious with fertilizer.** Skip the fertilizer entirely for at least the first week of the seedling stage. If you decide to use a fertilizer, try a very weak compost tea made from a bat guano fertilizer, or a highly diluted vegetative fertilizer. Be careful, as strong fertilizers will damage the tender seedling roots.

- **Keep an eye on the roots.** Some seedlings might outgrow their first container, so you'll need to transplant them into a larger container for the remainder of this growing stage to allow them to properly thrive and avoid becoming root bound.

⚞ HOW DO I IDENTIFY A ROOT-BOUND PLANT?

When a plant is root bound, it has outgrown its container and can no longer get all the nutrients and oxygen it needs to thrive. You can identify a root-bound plant by gently removing the plant from the container and looking at the root ball. If there's no soil visible, and only a mass of white roots, the plant is root bound and needs to be transplanted. A root-bound plant will exhibit either slow growth or no growth.

Transplanting during this stage may also become necessary if you sowed seedlings directly into containers, using more than one seed per container. In general, it's recommended that you don't sow multiple seeds in the same container, because transplanting tender seedlings is a shock, and it's easy to damage your seedlings in the process of untangling them from their neighbors. Also, you might end up having to cull out the weaker plants to allow stronger plants to flourish. When transplanting during this stage, refer to the tips and guidance in the following section. Though this information is centered on transplanting seedlings for the next stage of growth, it can also be applied to transplanting during the seedling stage.

PRO TIP: PREVENT "DAMPING OFF"

"Damping off" is a common affliction among seedlings and is, unfortunately, fatal. Damping off is caused by excessive growth of *Pythium* fungus on seedlings. It typically strikes seedlings that are planted in cold, wet conditions. Seedlings affected by damping off will suddenly wilt and collapse. There is no treatment for it. To prevent damping off, make sure to keep your seedlings moist—but not saturated—and warm.

One important thing to remember as you care for your seedlings is that they grow at naturally different rates, so don't be alarmed if some aren't growing as quickly as others. The seedling stage will last between one and three weeks, after which time they'll be ready to transplant into their more permanent home.

TRANSPLANTING SEEDLINGS

Since the seedling stage lasts between one and three weeks, it will be up to you to decide when your plants are ready to transplant into their more permanent homes (larger pots/containers either indoors or outdoors, depending on where you choose to grow your plants) for the vegetative growth stage. So, how will you know when it's time? With some experience, you'll learn to instinctively know when a plant is ready; however, as a beginner, a good rule of thumb is to wait until your seedling has put out at least three sets of mature leaves. If you think your plants still look too fragile to handle transplanting, trust your gut and wait another week.

HOW TO TRANSPLANT

If you used peat pellets or Rockwool cubes, transplanting your seedlings is fairly straightforward. Simply move each intact pellet or Rockwool cube into its new, larger home. You can transplant the pellet or seedling cube directly into 3" peat pots (using one pot per seedling). To do this, fill the new container partially with a basic soil mix, then drop the pellet or cube into the container and add more soil to finish filling the container. Water immediately after to moisten the new soil.

If you're using Rockwool cubes, you can also drop each seedling cube into a larger, unused cube, or even stack a seedling cube on top of another, unused cube. Don't worry: the roots will grow into the new Rockwool cube.

If you used the paper towel method to germinate your seeds, you will have already transplanted the sprouted seeds into containers, so unless they've outgrown their containers, you won't have to do this first transplant for mature growth. And if you started your seedlings directly in a container, your seedlings may also be ready for mature growth without needing to transplant them. If you do have to transplant, however (e.g., if the plants are root bound), use one of the following techniques to gently remove the seedling from its container:

- **The flip-and-tap method.** This is easiest to accomplish if your potting mix is nicely compact and a little on the dry side. To do this, carefully flip the container upside down and tap on the bottom until the entire root ball slides out into your hand. The seedling will be upside down, between your fingers. To transplant, drop the entire root ball into the new, larger container, then fill with potting mix up to the level of the original root ball. Try not to disturb the young roots.

- **The cutaway method.** To do this, simply cut away the bottom and even part of the sides of the original container. If you're using plastic containers, this may be difficult, so for that reason it's not recommended that you start seedlings in plastic. However, if you've started in peat pots or Styrofoam, it's easy to cut away part of the old container.

- **The last-resort dig and pray.** This method has the greatest risk of damaging your seedling's tender roots, so it should only be attempted if you have no other choice. This method involves "digging" the seedling out of its original container, keeping as many roots intact as possible, and transferring it to the new container. Common kitchen silverware can be used for this, for example, a butter knife and spoon combination to carefully lift the small root ball up and move it. Seedlings transplanted this way will need to be staked up with bamboo stakes in the new container.

In general, if you need to transplant during the seedling stage, you'll choose a container that is no more than 2" larger than the initial seedling container. If your plants are large enough to go into their final vegetative containers (meaning they have at least four sets of mature leaves), you can use standard gardening containers that range in size from 4" up to 1 gallon.

HARDENING OFF YOUR SEEDLINGS

If you're planning an outdoor grow, you'll need to "harden off" your seedlings before permanently relocating them outside. This isn't as necessary for indoor grows because you have total control over the environment, so your plants won't be dealing with challenges like wind, downpours, and most importantly, full sunlight. However, you still might have to harden off indoor seedlings before they are transplanted into your vegetative growing environment, if they look spindly, with narrow and weak stems.

Hardening off seedlings is a process by which you slowly introduce the young plants to the growing environment. Up until this point, they've been living a very pampered life, basking under fluorescent or LED lights, with high humidity and balmy temperatures. Exposing seedlings to strong winds and full sunlight without some kind of breaking in period would burn them. If you have a private space outside, like a balcony, start moving your seedlings outside for a few hours in the morning to get some sunlight. Gradually increase the time they're left outside until they are able to handle full afternoon sunlight. You can also gradually subject them to stronger airflow from a fan. As they transition into being ready for outdoor growth, you'll want to stake them with bamboo stakes. The whole process of hardening off your seedlings should only take between one and two weeks. At the end of this period, your plants will be fully acclimated to the outdoors and ready to be moved to their permanent location.

CLONING: THE SEEDLESS ALTERNATIVE

So far, this chapter has focused on growing marijuana from seeds, but you might be surprised to learn that much of the marijuana available today was never actually sprouted from seed. Instead, these plants started life as clones. As the name implies, a clone is an exact genetic replica of an original plant. Producing plants from clones is known as "asexual reproduction" because there is no fertilization involved and no sharing of genetic material. Instead, clones are started from cuttings taken from a "mother" plant that has been set aside by a grower for this very purpose.

As you become a more experienced grower, you can start your own mother plants to create clones. However, when you're just beginning, you still might be able to find clones. For instance, if you live in an area where you have easy access to other growers or collectives, clones are often shared among growers.

There are several advantages to starting your grow with clones, including:

- Less cost involved
- A lower failure rate
- Knowledge of the plant genetics
- A guaranteed female if the clone is from a female
- Faster flowering
- Ability to produce larger numbers of plants

HOW DO YOU MAINTAIN A MOTHER PLANT?

When it comes to cloning, you want the best mother plant possible. This makes sense when you consider that clones taken from this plant will have the exact same genetic profile as their mother. Mother plants should be kept in a vegetative state while you're using them for clones. Indoors, this is accomplished by maintaining the 18/6 photoperiod (18 hours of light and 6 hours of dark per every 24-hour period). When taking clones, select stems from the bottom of the plant, as these have the most natural rooting hormone present and are the most likely to succeed.

Although it may sound intimidating at first, cloning marijuana is actually easy, provided you have a mother plant you can take cuttings from. To make a clone, follow these simple instructions:

1 Choose a cutting that is at the bottom of the mother plant and has at least two leaf nodes above the cut.

2 Use a sterile blade to sever the stem of your chosen cutting at a 45-degree angle. (See Figure 2.2.) This will increase the surface area of viable root-forming cells. If you're taking many cuttings, you can temporarily store your cuttings in a glass or jar of fresh room-temperature water while you work to minimize the shock.

▲ Figure 2.2: Cutting

3 Once you have your cutting, use a sharp knife to scrape off the very outer layer of stem from the bottom ¼", then use the knife to split the stem ¼" up from the bottom. This will expose as much of the stem as possible to your chosen growing medium to encourage the growth of new roots.

4 When you're ready to plant, dip the cutting into a rooting hormone. There are many types of rooting hormone, available as both powders and gels at most garden centers and on online grow shops.

5 Plant the clone in the growing medium. The highest success rates are obtained by using rooting cubes made from Rockwool, but you can also use Jiffy cubes or even a plain, nonfortified peat mix. When you plant the clone, poke its sharp end down into the medium, then pinch around the top, or backfill the hole, to ensure the maximum contact between the clone and the growing medium. The cutting should be firmly positioned in the growing medium.

6 Place the clones under grow lights or on a sunny windowsill. You'll treat clones very similar to the way you treat seedlings, using either fluorescent or LED lighting to get them started. The light cycle for your indoor clones should be 18–24 hours of continuous light, using standard LED growing lights. For outdoor plants, use an 18/6 photoperiod to prevent early flowering when you move your plants outside.

Just like seedlings, clones appreciate a warm environment with high humidity. You can cover them with a clear dome to help increase the humidity and temperature, similar to the set-up you would use for seedlings. Cloning kits are also available that offer everything you'll need, including Rockwool cubes and cloning chemicals. Also remember that your clones don't have roots at first, so mist them regularly to keep them moist (but not soggy). Use plain water and skip any fertilizer. Once normal vegetative growth starts and the plant is putting out mature sets of leaves (usually in one to three weeks), you can start slowly introducing fertilizer at one-quarter strength.

Once you get the hang of cloning, you'll find that it is a great way to produce marijuana plants very quickly. You can use this method to easily produce dozens or even hundreds of female clones at a time.

PRO TIP: CLIP THE LEAF TIPS

Immediately after planting your clones, snip off the ends of the leaf tips. This will help prevent leaf yellowing and reduce the risk of your clones dying from shock. When regular growth resumes in one to three weeks, let new leaves grow naturally and do not snip them.

GETTING READY TO GROW: YOUR TOOL KIT

By this point, you've already acquired some of the tools you'll need to be successful in your growing journey, but as you head into the next phase (indoor or outdoor vegetative growth), there are a few items you'll likely need. Keep in mind that you may also need additional, more specialized gear for your particular grow, for example, the materials required to set up lights for a cabinet grow. The following is a basic list of necessary equipment:

- Gardening shears
- Gardening gloves (marijuana flowers produce copious amounts of sticky resin)
- Plant tags for tagging your strains
- A notebook for recording your grow
- Fertilizers and nutrients
- A soil pH meter

FIVE TIPS TO REMEMBER

Armed with your seedlings and these easy-to-find tools, you'll be ready to begin your indoor or outdoor grow. It's recommended that you read through the full chapter on whichever grow location you chose *before* starting, so you'll know what to expect. But first, be sure to look over the following takeaways from Chapter 2. These are the important things to keep in mind as you continue your journey in growing marijuana:

1 **Pick the best strain for your environment.** Decide if you're growing indoors or outdoors, then research the best strains for your choice.

2 **Good genetics equal good marijuana.** Buy the very best seeds you can afford.

3 **Pamper your seeds and seedlings.** Keep them in warm temperatures with high humidity.

4 **Be gentle.** Don't use any strong fertilizers on seedlings.

5 **Pay close attention.** Keep the plants moist but not soggy; be careful when tending to them so as not to damage any tender roots or stems.

CHAPTER 3

Growing Marijuana Indoors

For many people—including professional cultivators—growing marijuana indoors is the ultimate way to produce the powerful marijuana they want. And thanks to the growing number of resources, both physical and online, it's easier than ever to grow indoors. However, there are some unique challenges to growing good marijuana indoors, including providing the right type of light, and adequate water and nutrients. Plus, there's the important question of where to set up your grow.

Fortunately, this chapter is here to help! In the following sections, you'll discover tips and solutions for each of these indoor growing challenges and more. You'll also learn about the different growing setups you have to choose from, so you can make the best choice for your unique situation. Be sure to spend time reviewing the full chapter at least once before starting your grow so you'll be on the fast track to success.

GETTING STARTED

If you've ever looked at pictures of grow rooms online, you've probably seen huge rooms filled with impressive hanging lights, industrial ventilation, and professional irrigation. Of course, this can be intimidating as you think about your own grow. But don't fret! There are a few much simpler setups for growing marijuana indoors that anyone—whether a beginner or seasoned cultivator—can follow.

In the following sections, you'll explore each of these three easy options for indoor growing. Using any one of these methods will not only help you master certain growing techniques, but also allow you to get more acquainted with the marijuana plant itself. Note that these options can be used for the seedling, preflowering and flowering, and vegetative growth stages.

GROW TENTS

Grow tents are one of the newest options for indoor growing. As the name implies, a grow tent is a tent that's been specially designed for horticultural purposes. (See Figure 3.1.) Grow tents are common in professional marijuana cultivation because they make it easy for a grower to divide a single growing area into several different areas (one for cloning, one for vegetative growth, one for flowering, etc.).

Grow tents will work for any size grow, and you can easily find ones online that are small enough to fit into most spaces. Good grow tents come with reflective interior surfaces to maximize the amount of light available to your plants, and are built with fittings for ventilation, lights, and even CO_2 enrichment if you decide to use it.

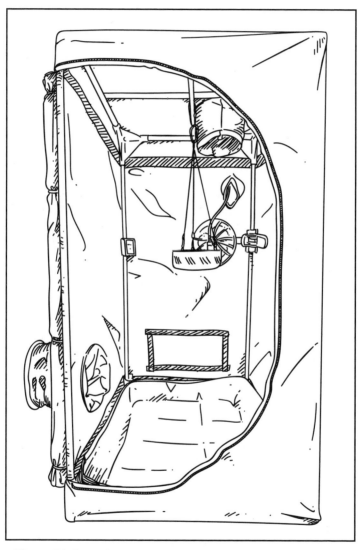

▲Figure 3.1: Grow Tent

In terms of their main advantages, grow tents are also:

- Self-contained, so you don't have to convert whole rooms into grow areas
- Relatively inexpensive, with serviceable tents available for under $100
- Designed for growing, so you don't have to modify or engineer anything
- Lightproof
- Odor-resistant
- Pest- and pet-resistant

When you're shopping for a grow tent, look for one that is built from durable materials, with higher-quality zippers and seams. It's also a good idea to get one with windows built into it so you can easily check on your marijuana plants without disturbing the growing environment.

Finally, look for a grow tent that offers sufficient height. A common mistake among new growers is to purchase a tent that doesn't allow for marijuana plants to get very tall, or makes it hard to keep hot lights away from your plants. You can grow marijuana in a 4' tent, however using a 6' or 8' tent will make the process easier.

PRO TIP: PICK AN OPTION THAT SUITS YOUR STRAIN

When you're setting up your indoor grow, pick a strain that is a good match for your chosen growing situation. A tent or cabinet is perfect for *indica*-dominant strains, as these plants are smaller in stature than *sativa*-dominant strains, and can be easily shaped to stay low enough to yield in a small space.

GROW CABINETS

Grow cabinets are very similar to grow tents, except they are typically made from a solid construction and often require some DIY skills to build yourself. Innovative indoor gardeners have made grow cabinets from old refrigerators, lockers, and armoires.

When you're designing a grow cabinet, make sure to plan for the following:

- Hanging lights that can be raised or lowered
- Lightproofing your cabinet so no light can escape and ambient light can't get in
- Holes for ventilation and air filtration
- A reflective interior surface
- Water management
- Electricity

If you don't want to make your own grow cabinet, you can easily buy one from a number of online manufacturers. At the higher end of the market, these cabinets (often called "grow boxes") offer features like set-it-and-forget-it automation (timers for watering and lights), hydroponic gear and lights, Bluetooth compatibility so you can monitor your crop on an Android or iOS device, and cloning shelves.

SPACE BUCKETS

Space buckets are one of the more modern trends in micro-grows (the practice of growing very small plants that still yield excellent marijuana). This method uses 5-gallon buckets to create a self-contained growing environment, complete with ventilation, lights, and room enough for one plant. With time and experience, you'll be able to regularly produce as much as 1 ounce of high-quality marijuana per space bucket, although your yield will likely be smaller at first. Some experienced space-bucket growers (called "bucketeers") can produce 2 ounces per grow! People also use space buckets to grow herbs, fruits and vegetables, and anything else that can be trained to a small space.

At first glance, these DIY projects can seem fairly complex, and it's true that there's a bit of a learning curve to designing and using a space bucket successfully. But that's part of the fun! And not to worry: Everything you'll need to know is laid out in this section. (Note: You can also skip part of the DIY involvement by purchasing pre-wired lights and fans online at www.spacebuckets.com. Then, simply disregard the rewiring instructions in the following section.)

Basic space buckets are made from two 5-gallon buckets that have been modified to provide a growing area with drainage and ventilation, plus an overhead light source using either compact florescent lights (CFLs) or UFO-style (round) LED lights. Space buckets can be modified for a hydroponic micro-grow, but for your first space bucket it's a good idea to start with a soil-based grow so you're only learning one new thing at a time. Most bucketeers also plant their marijuana in a separate smaller container inside the space bucket. This makes it easier to remove the plant and also to clean it between grows.

While there are a variety of great, easy-to-follow space bucket plans online (check out www.spacebuckets.com for more information), here is a list of the main components you'll need for a basic space bucket setup:

- Two 5-gallon buckets (with lids). (If you're planning on making spacers to create a taller space bucket, you'll want four buckets.)

- Lights (either small CFL light bulbs or a UFO-style LED light). (Depending on the lights you're buying, a 135 W or 180 W UFO light should be sufficient. You can also buy LED light strips to provide extra side lighting, but it's not strictly necessary. If you're using regular CFL bulbs, buy a fixture that can accommodate at least four lights and use 35 W bulbs.)
- Two PC 4" or 120 mm fans and a 12 V AC power connector. (A phone charger works great.)
- Reflective Mylar (if using buckets that are not white)
- Black duct tape
- Electrical tape and wiring nuts (if your fans or lights require rewiring)
- Power strip
- 24-hour timer (in case you want to automatically control the photoperiod)
- Zip ties or small screws
- Construction glue
- Marker (for drawing around a template)
- Drainage tray for your plant

You'll also need a few tools, including a drill and ¼" drill bit and large drill bits, box cutter–style knife, rotary tool or other bucket-cutting tool, measuring tape, and a wire stripper. Since you'll be using blades and possibly power tools, make sure to have all the safety gear you'll need on hand as well, including heavy gloves and safety glasses. Depending on your design, you might also need basic hardware, like small screws, so before you start building, make sure you've carefully planned every step.

PRO TIP: CUT SMALL, FIT TIGHT

Light control is essential to a good space bucket. When you're cutting holes for your ventilation fans and light fixtures, cut them slightly smaller than the template shapes. You want your fixtures to fit very snugly into the plastic. Ideally, they will support themselves; if they don't, you can use zip ties, construction glue, or screws to secure them further. And remember to thoroughly duct tape everything after it's secure to keep the bucket lightproof. At the minimum, you'll duct tape around any seams, but many bucketeers cover the entire space bucket with duct tape.

Steps to Creating a Space Bucket

Once you've gathered your materials and tools, you can get to crafting. The goal is to create the following parts that will be used in the final assembly: a main growing chamber (using one bucket), and a light hood (using the second bucket). You can also create spacers from two additional buckets if you want to make a larger space bucket. Before beginning, do plenty of research, seek expert guidance from a trusted source, and never undertake electrical work you do not have experience in.

Follow these easy steps to create your space bucket:

1 Flip bucket one over and drill drainage holes in the bottom. Aim for at least twelve holes, using a ¼" drill bit.

2 Using the glue, line the inside walls of bucket one with Mylar. It's easier to cut the Mylar into strips and glue them into place instead of trying to line the bucket with one large piece. (This

step isn't necessary if you're using white buckets, which reflect plenty of light on their own.)

3 Completely cover the outside of bucket one with a layer of black duct tape. It's only necessary to tape the sides of the bucket; don't tape the bottom of the bucket.

4 Using one of the PC fans as a template, draw an outline on one side of bucket one. This outline should be positioned within the bottom half of the bucket. Once this is done, turn the bucket to the opposite side and use the fan to draw another outline within the top half of the bucket.

5 Cut along the outlines you made in the previous step. These are your exhaust holes for the fans.

6 Fit your fans snugly into the two exhaust holes. The bottom fan should be positioned so it's blowing air *into* the space bucket, while the top fan should be positioned so it's pulling air *from* the space bucket. For now, don't permanently fasten the fans in place; just make sure they fit.

7 Create your light hood by first cutting off the top 5" of bucket two, making sure to include the bucket lid.

8 Depending on the type of lights you're using, you'll next cut holes in the bucket lid or sides of the bucket top (a.k.a. light hood) to mount the sockets or light fixtures. A 180 W UFO-style LED light makes this job easier, because you only need to cut one hole in the top of the bucket lid. If you're using CFL lights, you'll cut holes for the individual sockets, either in the top of the lid or the sides of the light hood. As with the fans, first draw the shapes of your cut-outs. Cut them slightly smaller than the drawn shapes; you want a nice, snug fit.

9 Fit the lights into the cut-outs.

10 Start wiring the fans by snipping off the phone charger's jack (the part you would plug into the phone).

11 Carefully isolate and strip about ½" of plastic from the ends of the two wires on each fan to expose the wire. Strip the same amount of plastic from the phone charger cable, so that wire is also exposed.

12 Twist the wire ends of the fans and charger cable together, fasten with a wire nut (following the label instructions), and secure the wire nut in place with electrical tape. At this point, you should be able to plug in the fans and they'll turn on.

13 Wire the lights. If you're using a halo light or an adapter socket for CFL bulbs, they should already have a plug you can use, so there's no wiring involved. If you bought separate sockets, follow the package instructions to wire these together. Again, the goal is to have lights you can plug in. (For more details on how to wire fans and lights, or answers to any questions you might have about wiring, look online for basic how-tos and tips, or ask a trusted professional.)

14 Place the light hood over bucket one. Your fans and lights aren't permanently fastened yet, so be careful as you place the light hood over bucket one (a.k.a. the growing chamber). The fit should be snug.

15 If you wanted to make a taller space bucket, you can now cut the top 5" from two more buckets (bucket lids removed) to make spacers. These spacers should be duct-taped to match your main growing chamber. They will stack on top of the main growing chamber and lift your light hood further away from your plant to provide more growing room.

16 Once the light hood and growing chamber have been fitted together, plug the fans and lights into the power strip and turn them on. You're looking to make sure everything is working.

17 Once you've confirmed everything is working, you can permanently attach the fans and lights using zip ties, small screws, or duct tape. This might require drilling additional holes through the bucket walls for zip ties or screws.

18 Once the fans and lights are firmly attached, use additional duct tape to seal off the seams around the fans and lights. This will help prevent loss of light.

19 If you're using a light timer, place it between the power strip and the wall socket so you can set the photoperiod.

And that's it! Your completed space bucket should be a multi-piece design: a main growing chamber topped with a light hood (plus spacers if you made these) and placed in a drainage tray. The chamber and light hood should fit easily together, but be stable enough that the light hood is snugly held in place. Ideally, when your plant is small, you won't need any spacers. As it grows, add spacers as needed to keep the plant from touching the lights.

PRO TIP: WATCH OUT FOR CHEAP UFO LIGHTS

UFO-style LED lights are perfect for space buckets because they are naturally low heat. Some even include fans, so they improve ventilation. But beware: Many UFO LED lights on the market are cheap and don't produce the warm light you want for growing. Do your research to find a good brand, and select a 135 W or 180 W light. If you're using multiple spacers to grow a larger plant, opt for a 180 W light. If you're planning to keep your plant small, a 135 W will suffice. In either case, you can also add LED light strips inside the bucket to provide a little extra light.

Once your space bucket is complete, you're ready to begin growing! Be aware that growing in a space bucket is not like growing in other environments, thanks to the smaller growing chamber. While experience will be your best teacher, here are some pointers to becoming a successful bucketeer:

- **Use one space bucket per plant.** This will prevent crowding and ensure that your plant gets as much light as possible.

- **Pick strains that are low-growing.** *Indica* varieties are a good choice.

- **Train your plant.** Use trimming and low-stress training (LST) techniques (see Chapter 6).

- **Keep in mind that it's better to flower early than late.** Your plants will stretch after you switch to a 12/12 light cycle, so it's best to start flowering a little earlier instead of waiting.

- **Disconnect the power supply when you're watering.** Remember that water and electricity *do not* mix.

PRO TIP: BE SAFE!

Space buckets are a great way to create a micro-grow, but it's important to practice safety when using them. When you're making your space bucket, if you do any wiring, make sure to use wire nuts and tape off all exposed wires. Also, many guides recommend taping your power strip to the side of your space bucket, but if it's possible to run your plugs a little farther away, it's safer to keep your power strip away from the bucket itself.

UNDERSTANDING INDOOR GROW LIGHTS

At some point very early in your indoor marijuana growing journey, you'll be asking this important question: "What type of lights do I need?" To fully understand the answer, it helps to have some basic knowledge of the color temperature and intensity of light, as these will be the two main elements involved in giving your plants the energy they need to flourish. Once you've taken a quick tour of these topics, you can make more informed decisions when it comes to purchasing your grow lights.

THE COLOR AND INTENSITY OF LIGHT

As you probably know, each color of the rainbow corresponds to a different wavelength of light, and each of these wavelengths falls on something called the "visible light spectrum." On this spectrum, each color has a color temperature (the appearance and feel of the light emitted) that is measured on the Kelvin scale. Blues are represented with higher readings, while the red and orange end of the spectrum has lower readings. To get a sense of what this means in practical terms, here are some Kelvin readings for different types of light:

- Blue sky, northern latitudes: 7,000–10,000 K
- A cool-white light bulb (incandescent or CFL): 6,000 K
- Metal halide (MH) light: 4,000 K
- Incandescent bulb: 2,600–3,100 K
- High-pressure sodium (HPS) light: 2,200 K

The Kelvin rating of different types of light bulbs is written on the package as the "CCT" (correlated color temperature).

Depending on its life-cycle stage, marijuana thrives between 1,500 K and 8,000 K. Flowering plants prefer more orange-red light with a lower Kelvin reading, while plants in vegetative growth prefer more blue-white light with a higher Kelvin reading. With this in mind, you can easily see why marijuana won't grow well with a typical incandescent light bulb. Instead, you need to provide a greater range of light that includes the warm red spectrum for flowering *and* the cool blue for vegetative growth.

You'll also want to make sure you can provide enough light intensity to power your plant's growth. The light intensity is the rate at which light energy is delivered to a unit of surface, and it is measured in watts and lumens. The wattage is the amount of energy needed to power the light source, while the lumens are the amount of light given off by that light source. The watts on a light bulb can range from anywhere between 2 and 1,500. The higher the watt number, the more lumens it produces, and the more energy it uses.

BUYING GROW LIGHTS

Now that you understand the main elements at play in lighting marijuana plants, it's time to look into purchasing your own grow lights for the vegetative growth, preflowering, and flowering stages of your plants. For most indoor grows, you'll focus on high-intensity discharge (HID) lights, which provide a greater range of light wavelengths and more watts than standard LED or CFL bulbs. (This doesn't include space bucket grows, which rely on LED or CFL lights to cut down the heat.)

The two most common types of HID lights are metal halide (MH) and high-pressure sodium (HPS) bulbs. You can use these lights in grow rooms, tents, or cabinets. The type of light you'll choose depends on how big your grow area is and how many plants you have. If you're setting up separate areas for flowering and vegetative growth, you might even use both, as HPS light is better for flowering and MH bulbs are perfect for vegetative growth. If you opt for only one kind of light, focus on HPS because it will help you grow larger buds.

HID lights are often sold in complete kits containing the following parts:

- **Bulb.** Bulbs are typically bare, to maximize their light output.

- **Reflector.** Reflectors take various shapes and sizes, but they are all designed to spread light.

- **Socket.** Sockets are typically attached to the reflector.

- **Ballast.** The ballast regulates the amount of electricity going into the bulb to light it and keep it lit. Ballasts can be either internal (attached to the socket) or external.

- **Timers.** Timers are used to control the photoperiod; you can set your lights to automatically turn on and off at certain times of the day.

PRO TIP: FOR SMALLER GROWS, THINK LED

If you're considering a smaller grow (typically a 4' × 4' growing area) that would require 400 W or less, you might be able to skip the HID lights entirely and instead invest in an LED light array. LED lights are cheaper than HID bulbs, consume much less electricity, and last much longer. The technology in this area moves very quickly, so do your research, but rest assured: For a typical small tent or cabinet grow, a high-quality LED light can do everything a HID light can do with less heat and less money.

Once you've decided on a type of light, you'll need to figure out how strong your light should be. HID lights are sold in different wattages, generally ranging from 20 W up to 1,500 W. As discussed previously, the higher wattage bulbs emit more usable lumens for your plants; however, they also emit more heat as they burn, so you have to keep them farther away from the plants (light intensity decreases as the light source moves farther away). In general, a single 600 W bulb should be plenty for a 4' × 4' growing area. You could also purchase two 400 W bulbs and spread them apart to provide more even light. If you're planning a larger grow (more than 5' × 5'), it's worth visiting a grow shop or online forum to get more insight into what lights will work best. Overall, you want to ensure you're delivering 3,000–4,000 lumens per square foot of growing area.

PROVIDING NECESSARY VENTILATION

Like all plants, marijuana relies on fresh air to grow well. Ventilation provides this fresh air for robust growth. It also helps maintain the perfect air temperature range of 75°F–80°F, removes humidity to reduce the risk of mold, and reduces the strong odors that marijuana generates.

So what makes a good ventilation system? The first thing to understand is that ventilation isn't referring to just standard fans that merely move air around and don't actually provide fresh air. A few oscillating fans are a good idea to help strengthen your plants' stems and branches, but if you're setting up any kind of contained grow, like a grow tent or even a space bucket, you'll want to install a system that pulls fresh air into the growing environment and vents stale air outside of it. The good news is that many grow tents come equipped with intake and exhaust ports for ventilation fans. And if you're setting up a larger grow room, there are lots of ways to vent your grow area, including installing vents in the walls or ceiling, or powered fans and carbon filters to remove air from your room.

To reduce discharge odors, you'll also want to install some kind of carbon filter in your ventilation system. There are many types of carbon filtration systems available on the market, as well as easy online tutorials on how to install them. To learn more about ventilation fans and carbon filters, as well as where to purchase them, check out the resources listed in the back of this book.

⇒ WHAT IS CO$_2$ ENRICHMENT?

Plants aren't like people: They "breathe" in carbon dioxide. Naturally, this means that plants with plenty of access to carbon dioxide tend to grow faster and get bigger than those with a weaker or less consistent source of carbon dioxide. More advanced growers will supply extra carbon dioxide to their grow area, usually with tanks of carbon dioxide. This practice is known as "CO$_2$ enrichment." It works well, but may be something you want to try after you have a few grows under your belt.

CHOOSING BETWEEN SOIL AND NO SOIL

Now that you've designed your indoor growing space, it's time to decide: soil or soilless? But first, let's talk about what soil is and isn't. Here, the word "soil" is being used to describe the bags of potting soil you typically see for sale at most garden stores. A good example is FoxFarm's Ocean Forest potting soil, which is made from products like composted peat or sphagnum, seaweed, and forest products like pine bark. Technically, this isn't the type of soil you'd find in an outside garden, but thanks to gardening tradition, bagged potting soil is still widely referred to as such, and it will be throughout this book whenever the term "soil" is used in the context of indoor growing. By contrast, a soilless grow generally refers to growing mediums that don't resemble soil at all. The most common types of soilless growing mediums include expanded clay pellets (known as "hydroton") and Rockwool. These are typically used in "hydroponics," in which nutrients are provided directly in the water rather than in a soil.

So, which one will you choose? When deciding what method will work best for your grow, the following are the main factors to take into consideration:

SOIL-BASED GROWING	SOILLESS GROWING
Less technical skill involved	More technical skill involved
Fewer plants in the same space	More plants in the same space
One plant per pot	All plants grown with the same solutions
Mistakes generally affect fewer plants	Mistakes can kill your whole crop at once
Less expensive	More expensive
Smaller yields per square foot	Higher yields per square foot
Slower flowering time	Faster flowering time

In general, those new to marijuana cultivation are advised to start with a soil-based grow. Don't worry about sacrificing quality or quantity: You can still grow top-notch marijuana in a soil-based container grow! Specifically, growing in soil is recommended for a beginning grower because you're focusing on one new thing—growing good marijuana—instead of learning how to grow good marijuana *and* how to manage a hydroponic system. Of course, if you are motivated to learn hydroponics, you can certainly start there (check out Chapter 4 for a basic guide).

The following sections will break down soil-based grows. Again, the decision of whether you use this method or a soilless method (again, see Chapter 4 on hydroponics) is completely up to you and what you feel is best for your growing situation.

GROWING IN SOIL

Once you have the lights and grow area set up, you're ready to start growing! In this section, you'll explore the main components of soil-based indoor growing, from what soils to choose from, to how and when to water your plants. For your first grow (or more), let's assume that you're not rigging any type of automatic irrigation system and that you have regular access to your plants to water and pay attention to them.

CONTAINERS

You can grow marijuana in any type of container as long as it has good drainage. Most indoor growers use black plastic nursery containers because they're cheaper and lighter than plant pots made from materials such as ceramic or clay. You can also use fabric containers, which are slightly porous and allow more air to reach the soil, or specialized Air-Pot containers, which have holes in the side to increase oxygen levels near the root zone. While there may be advantages to spending more on specialized containers, it's recommended that you start with simple black plastic containers.

When purchasing your containers, you'll also need to make sure they are large enough with adequate growing space. Marijuana has a large, spreading root system, so a healthy plant needs plenty of room to grow underground. Although it's possible to grow marijuana in smaller containers (down to 1 gallon or even smaller if you're using specialized trimming techniques), 3-gallon containers are recommended.

The shape of the container isn't necessarily important to the plant, so you can get a shape that fits your grow room. For example, if you're planning on using an advanced training and trimming method like sea of green (SOG) or screen of green (SCROG)—which are both covered in Chapter 4—you might want square, taller containers that fit together well and still provide room for roots. These methods are more common in hydroponics, but can be used with any type of grow.

Finally, you'll need trays or some other way to remove excess water that drains from the bottom of the containers. In general, it's a bad idea to leave any excess water in your growing area; it will raise the humidity as it evaporates and increase the risk of bud rot and mold.

POTTING SOIL

Soil is the place where your marijuana will actually grow, so this is not the place to pinch pennies. Instead, it's recommended that you purchase a high-quality potting mix that provides structure for the growing roots, good water retention, and excellent drainage. A high-quality mix should feel light and fluffy before it's watered.

Typical ingredients in a high-quality soil mixture can include:

- Sphagnum peat moss
- Pine bark fines
- Forest products
- Vermiculite and/or perlite
- Soil amendments

If you have some background knowledge in container gardening, you can easily mix up your own container mix with the ingredients listed, but this isn't necessary. There are many excellent bagged potting soils available on the market. FoxFarm's Ocean Forest is a particular favorite among many marijuana growers; this soil mix is a potent blend of forest products, composted sphagnum peat, organic nutrients like earthworm castings and bat guano, fish emulsion, and other ingredients that guarantee good drainage and structure.

As a last note, remember to avoid using the same enhanced soil on your seedlings that you use for the main grow. Many of these enhanced soils are too "hot" for seedlings and will burn their roots with excess fertilizer. Fertilizer for both indoor and outdoor soil-based grows will be covered in depth in Chapters 6 and 7, where you'll dive deeper into the marijuana plant's nutrient needs at different stages of its life cycle. It is recommended that you review these chapters before beginning your grow.

PRO TIP: DON'T RECYCLE (POTTING SOIL) OR USE DIRT

When you're contemplating spending $20 or $30 on a single bag of high-quality potting soil, it can be tempting to look for ways to cut corners. Maybe you're thinking it would work just as well to go outside and dig up some of your excellent black dirt from the veggie patch. Don't. It won't work. There is no comparison between the soil found in your garden and the specialized potting soil blends made for containers. Outdoor soil is heavier and won't drain well, and it may have serious nutrient deficiencies. Also, outdoor soil is likely to be loaded with eggs and pests that can seriously damage or destroy your indoor marijuana crop. Just as importantly, don't attempt to recycle used potting soil after a successful grow. Simply compost the old soil or fold it into your outside garden; your veggies *and* your next marijuana crop will both be grateful.

WATER

Water your marijuana with room-temperature or cool water: between about 68°F and 75°F.

Water quality can also affect your crop, especially if you're using well water or tap water that has dissolved salt or solids in it. If you can afford it and have the room, a reverse osmosis filter will provide the best quality water for your marijuana because it will remove any chemicals and contaminants from your water. If you can't, or you don't want to invest in another piece of equipment, you can use tap water. Just remember that water is not a substitute for fertilizer: No matter what type of water you use, you'll still need to feed your plants.

How much water your plants require depends on their size and your growing environment. In general, marijuana likes uniformly moist soil. Your soil should never be allowed to dry out completely, and it should never feel spongy or soggy. In the beginning, your smaller plants will require less water, but you may still need to water once daily or every other day. Lack of water will present itself in a wilted plant. As your plants get larger and move into successively larger containers, they'll need more water. However, thanks to the carrying capacity of the soil, larger plants may be able to go two or three days between waterings.

Here are a few tips to keep in mind when you're watering your marijuana plants:

- **Water adequately.** Water until the water runs freely from the bottom of the container into your drainage tray.

- **Empty the drainage trays after you water.** Never let your plants sit in water; this will encourage root rot.

- **Water the soil, not the plants.** Never pour water directly onto the developing flowers, as this will encourage bud rot and damage the flowers.

❋ WHEN TO WATER?

There's no ironclad rule on how often you should water your marijuana plants. Instead, look for these telltale signs:

- The first approximate ½"–¾" of the soil is dry when you poke your finger down into it.

- The container feels light when you pick it up. (For comparison, pick one up right after watering to see how it feels.)

- The leaves are wilting. If you're very concerned about watering, you can buy a water meter to measure the water content in the soil. These devices are widely available at garden centers and online.

FIVE TIPS TO REMEMBER

Now that you have the basics for indoor soil-based growing down, you're ready to dive deeper a little with an introduction to hydroponics and other soilless indoor growing techniques. But before you do, be sure to review the following main tips from this chapter. Keep these in mind when starting your soil-based indoor grow:

1 **Let there be light (and fans).** Provide adequate light and ventilation for your grow area; follow the information in this chapter, and feel free to do more research online when buying

equipment. Seek expert guidance from a trusted source before setting up any system.

2 **One pot, one plant.** This will ensure that each plant has enough room to grow, reduce the risk of disease or pests, and make it easier to remove individual plants affected by pests or disease.

3 **Don't pinch pennies.** Use the best potting soil you can afford; never use regular garden soil.

4 **Practice good watering.** Water the soil regularly and deeply, until water runs from the bottom of the container.

5 **Remove water from the drainage tray immediately.** Never let your plants sit in water, as it can cause root rot and increase humidity in your grow area.

CHAPTER 4

Hydroponics

By now, you've read a little about hydroponics, the soilless indoor growing method that uses nutrients in a water solution to grow your plants. This technique can seem intimidating at first, but it's quite doable, and for many marijuana growers, it's the only way to get the results they want. In fact, there are many advantages to hydroponics, like robust root growth, quicker flowering times, and larger buds. And with the widespread availability of all-in-one kits, a lot of the guesswork of setting up your first system is eliminated. Of course, a kit isn't all there is to it, and that's where this chapter comes in!

In the sections that follow, you'll find everything you need to know about creating and successfully using hydroponics in your marijuana grow. From the types and parts of this system, to ensuring it is doing its job effectively, this chapter is your crash course on hydroponics. If you've decided to go with a soil-based growing method to start (recommended for beginning growers), feel free to skip this information. As you become a more experienced grower, you may later decide to try your hand at hydroponics. Also keep in mind that while this chapter focuses on indoor hydroponics, you can certainly use this method in outdoor marijuana grows, though it is less common.

BASIC HYDROPONICS

As outlined previously, hydroponics is the act of growing plants without soil. This means you'll be providing water, nutrients, and oxygen directly to the root systems, instead of relying on the roots to absorb these elements from the growing medium. (Hydroponic marijuana grows begin once the seedling is ready to transplant for vegetative growth—unless you are growing the seedlings in Rockwool, or growing clones.) However, growing hydroponically doesn't mean there's no growing medium involved (unless you're using an aeroponic system, in which the plant roots grow in open air and are misted with nutrient-rich water). Instead, you'll use a medium that provides structure for the roots and may have some water retention, but does not supply any nutrients. The most common growing mediums for hydroponics include:

- Rockwool
- Expanded clay pellets
- Vermiculite
- Perlite
- Coconut coir

CATEGORIES OF HYDROPONIC SYSTEMS

There are two broad categories of hydroponic systems. Following, you'll find an outline of each type:

1 **Passive.** This is the simplest system by design, but it can also be tricky to perfect. In a passive system, the plants are suspended above a nutrient solution. Water is supplied to the plant either through the roots directly, as they dangle down into the solution,

or through a wick that pulls water up from the nutrient solution into the growing medium as the plant needs it. One common issue that can arise with this system (the wick system) is either lack of water (because the plant sucks up water faster than the wick can transport it) or too much water (because the growing medium soaks up too much and becomes spongy).

2 Active. In this hydroponic system, the nutrient solution is pumped into the plants' growing area, where it is delivered to the root zone. Most hydroponic systems used in marijuana culture are active. Common types of active systems include ebb and flow, drip irrigation, nutrient film technique (NFT), and deep water culture (DWC). Each of these will be covered in more detail later in this chapter.

THE PARTS OF A HYDROPONIC SYSTEM

No matter what types of hydroponic systems you're interested in, most of them will share common parts that are stored in the grow tent, grow cabinet, or other growing space you set up. Here are the basic elements of a hydroponic system:

- **Container.** Your marijuana plants need to grow in some type of container to provide support. In hydroponics, containers range from standard plastic containers to net pots to long, wide tubes with holes for net pots or Rockwool cubes to be inserted.

- **Growing medium.** The most common types of hydroponic systems use some kind of soil-less growing medium, such as coconut coir, Rockwool, or hydroton-expanded clay pellets.

- **Reservoir.** The reservoir is where your water and nutrient solution is held. In most hydroponic systems, the reservoir is a closed system. This means that after the plants are watered, excess solution flows back into the reservoir and is used again. This helps preserve your nutrient solution.

- **Pump.** In an active system, a pump is used to move the water from the reservoir to the plants' growing containers. Passive systems don't require pumps.

- **Air stones.** Depending on your system, it might use air stones to aerate the solution in the reservoir.

- **Timers.** Because there is little growing medium (or in the case of aeroponics, no growing medium) used, roots can dry out very quickly in hydroponic systems. Timers are used to guarantee that the growing solution is delivered precisely when it's needed.

- **Measuring instruments.** These will include tools to measure the EC (electrical conductivity) and TDS (total dissolved solids), along with the pH and temperature of your water.

Exactly how these different components work together depends on the type of hydroponic system you choose. In the next sections, you'll find more details on the most common types of hydroponic systems, along with the pros and cons of each. Keep in mind, however, that many experienced growers often modify different systems, blurring the lines between growing methods to create their own.

Also, be aware that this is meant as an overview of hydroponic systems, not a complete guide to troubleshooting a specific system. For more information and answers to any questions you may have when creating and using your own hydroponic system, visit a hydroponics shop to talk to experts, or check out helpful forums online. Once you get the hang of it, you'll find this can be an incredibly rewarding way to grow marijuana.

✺ TO BUILD OR TO BUY?

You'll find many types of hydroponic systems available online as full kits. There's no question that these kits are a great way to get started, but be sure to do your research and read reviews to make sure the kit you buy is well constructed and appropriate for plants as large and robust as marijuana. In many systems, you may need to upgrade elements like pumps and air stones. Cost is also a consideration; preconstructed kits can be expensive, and you might find that you can build a very similar system for a fraction of the price.

DEEP WATER CULTURE

Deep water culture (DWC) is one of the most common hydroponic systems. It can be used for a large-scale grow or for just a few plants. Deep water culture is a passive system that involves suspending a plant in a net pot over a reservoir so its roots can dangle down into the nutrient solution. The net pot is filled with an inert growing medium, such as expanded clay pellets, to provide structure, while the roots are free to grow straight down into the water. (See Figure 4.1.) This might seem counterintuitive, as under normal conditions plants will die if their roots are waterlogged; however, this problem is solved in deep water culture by putting an aerator or air stone in the reservoir to keep the water bubbling.

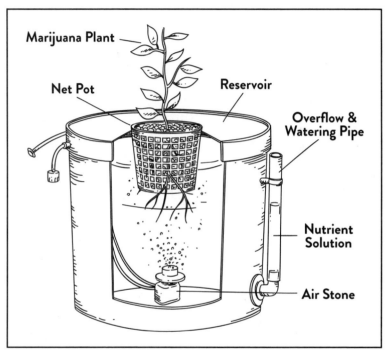

▲ Figure 4.1: Deep Water Culture System

A DWC system can be set up with just one plant, or you can use a modular system that grows multiple plants suspended over one reservoir. You can also link multiple DWC containers to a common reservoir and pump water through them, although this would be considered an active system because it uses pumps. Under proper circumstances, a DWC system will provide astounding results, with plants generating enormous masses of roots and heavy, pungent buds. Success with a DWC system involves:

- Keeping the water the right temperature (less than 72°F and greater than 63°F).

- Providing enough aeration in the water to feed the roots.

- Keeping the water in the right pH zone (around 5.5–6.5 pH).

- Providing the right nutrient strength in the reservoir. Once a DWC system is set up, it's relatively low maintenance, other than maintaining the reservoir. The pumps (if you're using them) and aerators will run 24 hours a day. Deep water culture is a natural place to start your hydroponic gardening, since the system is easily expandable and relatively simple to set up.

HOW DO YOU MEASURE PH IN A HYDROPONIC RESERVOIR?

Maintaining the right pH in your reservoir is essential for successful hydroponics. Hydroponic marijuana grows best between 5.5 and 6.5 pH. Fortunately, measuring the pH (a measure of acidity and alkalinity) of your reservoir is easy with a pH measuring kit. They are available as liquid test kits or strips, or you can buy an electronic pH meter. If your pH is out of range, you can easily correct it with a "pH up" or "pH down" solution. These are also available online, or through a hydroponics shop. Follow label instructions to add them to your reservoir.

EBB AND FLOW

Ebb and flow systems are popular, low-maintenance options for hydroponic growing. Although you can easily find ebb and flow kits online, many people build their own, thanks to the simplicity of the design.

In a basic ebb and flow system, plants are suspended over a deep tray, allowing their roots to fill up the tray. In most cases, the plants are anchored in net pots filled with some kind of inert growing medium. The reservoir is located below the tray and connected to it with a tube and pump. On a preset schedule, the pump activates and floods the tray with nutrient solution from the reservoir, feeding the plants. The tray is equipped with an overflow tube that drains back down into the reservoir so the tray doesn't overflow. In between floodings, the roots dry out and have access to oxygen.

This type of system is perfect if you want to grow a large number of shorter plants and are planning to trim and train your plants. The sea of green technique (discussed in detail later in this chapter) can be used with an ebb and flow system to create a canopy of heavy buds.

PRO TIP: WATCH YOUR RESERVOIR TEMPERATURE

The most important thing to remember when using a hydroponic system is to keep your reservoir water at the right temperature. As mentioned previously, the ideal reservoir should be no warmer than 72°F and no colder than 63°F. This temperature range prevents algae formation and makes it easier for your plants to uptake nutrients. If you're growing in a warmer environment, you can add a commercial chiller to your reservoir to keep it from becoming too hot. These are available through hydroponics shops and online retailers.

DRIP IRRIGATION

Also known as a "top-feed system," this type of hydroponic system is simple in theory but can be a little more involved than other systems. It's very similar to the DWC system, except that instead of roots dangling down into a nutrient solution, the nutrient solution is pumped through tiny feeder tubes and dripped or microsprayed onto the surface of the growing medium, which is typically coconut coir or expanded clay pellets. Runoff from the watering is collected and returned to the reservoir.

These are great systems, but they can be finicky. With a lot of small tubing and microirrigation parts (sprayers and drippers), you'll have to frequently check to make sure nothing is clogged and all of your plants are getting adequate water and nutrition. Apart from this, reservoir maintenance is similar to other active hydroponic systems.

It's interesting to note that while a drip irrigation system is technically hydroponics, if you're growing in coconut coir grow bags or with a sphagnum-based mix, it also looks like a typical soil grow. In fact, the line between hydroponics and indoor soil-based growing is often blurred so much that it can be hard to tell them apart.

⟫ WHAT ARE EC AND TDS?

As you look deeper into the world of hydroponics, you will see mentions of "EC" and "TDS." Electrical conductivity (EC) and total dissolved solids (TDS) are measurements of the amount of dissolved solids in your nutrient solution. Assuming pure water has an EC of 0, any measurement over 0 is an indication of how strong your nutrient solution is. TDS is calculated using the EC number, and is expressed as parts per million (ppm). Both can be measured with simple devices that are inserted into the solution. If you plan on becoming proficient at growing hydroponic marijuana, you'll want to become acquainted with the different ideal EC and TDS readings for the different systems. Fortunately, most hydroponic nutrient manufacturers make it easy: They publish the ideal EC and TDS values for different growth stages online and on the packages.

NUTRIENT FILM TECHNIQUE

The nutrient film technique, or NFT, is one of the most popular hydroponic systems available today and is standard in all types of hydroponic gardening. Like the ebb and flow system, an NFT system uses a pump to circulate a nutrient solution around the roots of a plant. In the NFT system, however, the plants are planted in tubes (often called "gullies"), and instead of flooding and draining the root zones, the water is continuously pumped through the gullies to constantly bathe the roots in solution. To keep things flowing, the gullies are mounted on a table or rack at a slight angle.

The system is a closed loop: Water is pumped from the reservoir to the top of the gully, then passes through the gully and back into the reservoir under the table.

In a typical NFT system, plants are held in Rockwool cubes that are placed in net pots and suspended in holes along the top of the gully, with their roots filling the gully beneath and getting constant access to the growing solution. In a well-balanced NFT system, the flow of water through the bottom of the gully will be very shallow—hence the term "nutrient film"—and the roots will have enough room to grow without piling up and blocking the flow.

An NFT system is ideal for smaller plants, and can be paired with either the sea of green or screen of green technique (explained in more detail later in this chapter).

ADVANCED INDOOR GROWING TECHNIQUES

Like with everything else, experience will be your best teacher in understanding hydroponics, and a little practice will help you master it in no time.

Growing hydroponically may also change the way you train and shape your plants. With systems like NFT or ebb and flow, you're likely to be growing many smaller plants in close proximity instead of larger plants in separate containers. For maximum yield, this means you'll be packing your plants very close together, then training them to form an even canopy under the lights, so each plant will get the same amount of light. You'll also be trimming your plants to produce only one or two large colas per plant, instead of letting them get bushy. In the following sections, you'll learn more about the two most popular techniques of training plants to achieve this affect. Also note that these training techniques are not limited to hydroponics: You can use them with a soil-based grow, especially if you have limited room in your growing space.

SEA OF GREEN

The sea of green (SOG) technique revolutionized indoor marijuana growing, thanks to its ability to pack a large number of small plants into a small growing space and turn out a harvest very quickly. The idea behind the SOG technique is to plant your entire growing area with clones (see Chapter 2 for more detail on working with clones), packing them as closely together as possible and triggering flowering very quickly to limit their size.

When you're attempting a SOG grow, don't try growing from seedlings. Not only do they take too long in vegetative growth, but also, they will grow to different heights naturally. In the SOG technique, you want the most even canopy possible. SOG also works best with *indica* and *indica*-dominant strains because they're smaller, and SOG does particularly well with hydroponic systems like NFT and ebb and flow, which make it easy to pack plants close together and still get access to your canopy. Popular strains like Northern Lights and White Widow are excellent candidates for SOG.

Again, experience will be your best teacher with this technique. Don't be surprised if things don't go exactly as planned during your first try, or you don't harvest as much as you'd hoped. The best thing you can do is keep detailed grow records for improving future grows. Record the strain, the length of time you kept it in vegetative growth before flowering, how much the plants stretch (i.e., how much they grow after you induce flowering) during the flowering stage, and other details that you can use in your next grow.

For success in the SOG technique, follow these simple tips:

1   Plant your grow area with clones, packing them as closely together as possible. It's best to use tall, square containers. With this approach, you can grow up to ten plants per square foot. Don't allow more than 1 square foot per individual plant.

2   Allow your new clones about two weeks to develop healthy roots, then two weeks of vegetative growth before stimulating flowering by switching to a 12/12 light cycle.

3   Plan your lighting scheme to evenly cover your growing area. If you see that some plants are growing faster than others, it's likely because they are getting more light.

4   You're focusing on the top cola only in SOG, but in many SOG grows, no trimming is necessary, since you're forcing flowering so fast that the plants don't have time to branch out. If you do see branching and need to trim, you can clone the cuttings.

5   No staking (or minimal staking) should be required. If the plants are close enough, the canopy should support itself as the plants lean against each other. If staking is necessary, use bamboo to support individual plants.

6   Once you've forced flowering, treat them as any other marijuana plants, with the same nutrient requirements and harvest techniques described in the other chapters of this book.

In all, from transplanting to harvest, the SOG method can produce a crop in about ten to twelve weeks, depending on the strain.

SCREEN OF GREEN

The screen of green (SCROG) technique is closely related to the SOG method, with a few key differences. In this approach, fewer plants are packed into the same space (*at least* 1 square foot per plant, instead of *no more* than 1 square foot per plant), where they are allowed to grow up through a screen that is suspended over the growing space. You can make this screen from regular chicken wire, concrete reinforcing wire, or monofilament fishing line. When the plants hit the screen, they are trained to bend over and grow along the screen horizontally, sending branches out in different directions. When it's time to flower, the plants will produce multiple smaller colas from branches that have been growing laterally.

SCROG is a good choice for *indica*-dominant varieties, which fit well in the smaller growing space, but you can also grow *sativa*-dominant varieties. For *indica* strains, position the screen about 1' above the growing surface. For *sativa* strains, position the screen about 2' above the growing surface.

Training your marijuana is simple once it hits the screen: Gently bend the branches and tie them to the screen with twine or any type of tie. In this technique, you're encouraging bushy plants, so you'll likely do some pruning and topping (explained in more detail in Chapter 6) during the grow to get the shape you want.

The main advantage to SCROG versus SOG is that it uses fewer plants and is easier to use with *sativa*-dominant varieties, because it allows the plants to get bigger. Like SOG, however, it will take a little time and practice to master. Keep good records, stick with the same strain for one or two grows, and don't give up!

FIVE TIPS TO REMEMBER

It's true there is a learning curve to hydroponics, but anyone can develop the skills to be a hydro gardener! And hydroponics isn't just for your marijuana grow: You can use the same experiences and lessons to cultivate other plants as well, including vegetables. Here are the main tips that will help ensure your success:

1 **Start simple.** Don't invest in a huge and expensive system in the beginning. Start with a simple DWC system (as opposed to multiple buckets linked together) or a small NFT table and learn from there.

2 **Make sure your pump is the right size.** For example, growers are often tempted to pump too much water through their NFT systems, thinking that more must be better. This encourages root rot. Instead, aim for a very thin layer of water in your NFT system.

3 **Take good notes.** Record your reservoir strength, feeding schedules, flowering and light schedules, strain information, and harvest. You might think you'll remember this information from grow to grow, but you'll be surprised how often you return to your grow journal to answer a question you thought you'd already solved.

4 **Follow the nutrient schedule from your fertilizer manufacturer.** Leading companies like General Hydroponics have taken out a lot of the guesswork involved in hydroponic gardening.

5 **Make sure you can maintain an ideal temperature.** Hydroponic reservoir water should be cool, between 63°F and 72°F.

CHAPTER 5

Growing Marijuana Outdoors

After learning about all of the advantages to growing indoor marijuana, as well as the variety of grow methods available to choose from, you might wonder, "Why even bother with an outdoor grow?" Don't disregard it just yet! Outdoor marijuana has a number of great benefits that make it worthwhile, the principal being its taste. In fact, many people swear that outdoor marijuana has a more complex, fuller flavor profile than indoor marijuana—and it turns out they're onto something. Marijuana flowers produce many compounds, one of the most important being terpenes, or the aromatic oils that give the plant its distinctive flavor profile. And terpene production is enhanced under natural sunlight. Powered by this pure sunlight, outdoor marijuana plants can also grow to massive proportions. A single outdoor plant may yield several pounds of high-quality bud!

Growing marijuana outdoors might just be the right fit for you, and with the help of this chapter, you can cultivate powerful, healthy plants in no time. Here, you'll first learn about the different factors you'll need to consider when planning and executing a successful outdoor grow. Once you understand the main things that will affect your grow, you'll then explore the best strains for outdoor growing. Finally, you'll dive into the details of planting and growing your chosen strain. Be sure to read through the chapter in full before beginning your grow.

UNDERSTANDING YOUR CLIMATE

As an outdoor grower, you will need to first become well acquainted with the environment your plants will be grown in. This means knowing when the temperatures will be warm enough to transplant your crop, when the photoperiod will shift and send your plants into flowering, how much rainfall your plants will get, and when you'll need to harvest by to avoid cold damage to your crop.

If you live in the US, a good place to start understanding your environment is with the US Department of Agriculture (USDA) Plant Hardiness Zone Map. (You can find versions of this online by simply searching for "USDA Plant Hardiness Zone Map.") This rainbow-hued map shows the average annual minimum winter temperatures in the US, on a scale of 1–13. States with a hotter climate and a lower average winter temperature have a higher rating, while states with colder winters have a lower rating. Similar maps for countries outside of the US can also be found online by searching for "Plant Hardiness Zone Map" with the name of the location you plan to grow in.

In addition to using the map, you should also know the approximate date of your area's first frost (if you have one) and when it's safe to plant following the colder months. This information will help you plan your garden so you can maximize your growing time. In most areas of the US, marijuana can be planted outside in March or April and harvested in September. Keep in mind that while this is the most common growing season, there can be some variation depending on your strain and location.

PRO TIP: CONSULT YOUR COUNTY EXTENSION OFFICE

As you're researching your environment, don't neglect your local county extension office (if you live in the US). County extension offices are a great resource for knowledge about the local environment and planting conditions. Your county extension office can help you understand what type of soil is in your area, what the typical rainfall and temperature patterns are, and what are common pests, as well as give great advice on proper fertilizing and land management.

SOIL TYPE

Dirt is not just dirt. Soil types vary wildly across each region, and they can have a profound effect on your marijuana plants. In many cases, you will want to improve the soil to ensure healthier plants. Many growers working with heavy, clay-type soils dig holes for their marijuana plants, then fill the holes with high-quality dirt. Others use organic farming techniques like crop rotation and companion planting to improve the quality of their soil year after year, crop after crop.

The USDA recognizes twelve different types, or orders, of soil, but you can simplify this further by breaking them down into the five main types that are outlined in the following list. While the information in this section discusses each soil in terms of its location in the US, these classifications are found globally. You can find more information on soil types in different countries online:

- **Clay.** This soil is heavy and dense, with poor air circulation. It also has high water retention. Clay soil should be amended with organic matter including compost or composted manure to improve drainage and make it lighter. This type of soil is common along the coasts and wetlands.

- **Sandy.** Sandy soil has a higher proportion of sand than any other soil type. It also has better drainage than clay and isn't as heavy, but is often nutrient deficient. Improving sandy soils can be challenging, because organic materials like compost and peat wash away easily. If you grow in sandy soil, you will need to improve your plot every year, preferably with a rich compost. Sandy soils are found in deserts and near the coast.

- **Silty.** Silty soil is a combination of sandy soil and clay. It can feel very light and floury when it's dry, but heavy and thick when it's wet. Silt can be very fertile, with good drainage and moisture-holding capacity. A challenge with silty soil is holding it in place. You can improve your silty soil by amending it with compost. Silty soils are common in the Great Lakes and Midwest region, where ancient glaciers deposited silt as they retreated.

- **Peaty.** Peaty soil is formed from decomposing plant materials in a watery environment. It is a very fertile, rich soil, but often has poor drainage. If you have a peat-based soil, you can improve it by adding some type of structure, such as mulch or bark. Peaty soils are found in and around marshlands and other wet areas.

- **Loamy.** Loamy soil is a combination soil. It contains sand, clay, and silt in some proportion, usually with organic forest materials mixed in. Loam is a superior soil for growing crops due to its water-retention and drainage properties, as well as high organic matter. Loam feels crumbly and rich and is common east of the Mississippi.

The soil in your area might fall into one of these categories, but it might also have other unique characteristics that can affect your crop. One of the most important of these characteristics is your soil pH. (Remember that pH is a measure of acidity and alkalinity.) Marijuana thrives in neutral soil, so you want to aim for soil that is near to a reading of 7 or is slightly acidic (overall, the optimal range for growing outdoors is 6.0–7.0 pH). Soils that are high in lime typically have a higher pH, while soils that have been intensively farmed or are rich in decaying organic matter tend to more acidic. Details for how to deal with each of these situations are found later in this chapter.

Overall, you'll want to grow your marijuana in rich, loam-type soil with good drainage, a neutral pH, and nice water retention. If your growing soil isn't naturally this type, don't worry: There are plenty of easy ways to improve soil quality.

PRO TIP: KNOW YOUR SOIL

If you're planning to grow more than a few plants outside, it might be a good idea to invest in a soil sample analysis. Often offered through your local extension office, a soil analysis will give you excellent information on the composition of your local soil, as well as its pH and possible pests.

RAINFALL AND HUMIDITY

Just like there's no substitute for real sunlight, there's no doubt that fresh, clean rainwater is optimal when growing your own plants. The issue, however, is making sure you have enough (or not too much) at the right times.

As generations of farmers have learned through experience, you can't always count on regular rainfall. It's likely you will have to provide some irrigation for your outdoor marijuana crop. This is especially true in the beginning of the grow, when your plants are smaller and still getting established. If your plants are in your yard or are otherwise easily accessible, this can be easily accomplished through manually watering. If your plants are farther away, however, or you're growing on land you don't own, your options will differ. While professional growers often rig up irrigation systems with pumps, pipes, and reservoirs, this may not be practical for a beginning grow. If possible, try to visit your plants weekly and bring water with you. This may be enough when combined with regular seasonal rainfall.

Humidity is also an important factor in marijuana's growth, especially later in the plant's life cycle. This will be discussed in is greater detail in Chapter 7, but marijuana flowers are vulnerable to fungi—particularly mold. This mold is encouraged by high humidity. If you're growing in a region with high humidity during the months your crops will be flowering, make sure you factor this into your choice of marijuana strains. In this case, it's recommended that you start with a tropical *sativa*-dominant strain that has been bred to handle high heat and humidity. Some strains known for mold resistance include Amnesia Haze, Strawberry Sour Diesel, and Strawberry Cough. Seed banks and online forums will have more information on strains with better mold resistance.

PRO TIP: TRY A RAIN BARREL

A rain barrel is a simple device that is designed to catch and store rainwater for watering your plants. Rain barrels are readily available in garden centers, or through local agricultural co-ops. A typical rain barrel has a 55-gallon drum, a lid with a screen to prevent the water from getting infested, and a hose bib on the bottom that fits a standard garden hose. These ecologically friendly containers are a great way to ensure a more even supply of fresh water. If you are growing in your yard, you can hook a rain barrel up to a downspout and capture excess rainwater. Just be sure to check regulations in your area before making a purchase.

SEASONAL PHOTOPERIOD

By now, you have learned that marijuana is sensitive to the photoperiod, or the amount of light versus darkness in a regular 24-hour day. Outdoor growers can't control the photoperiod like indoor growers can, so you'll rely on the naturally changing photoperiod to send your plants into flowering.

In most areas of the US, your plants will automatically go into flower in the late summer and continue flowering into the fall. If you happen to be growing in an area in the US—or outside of the US—with less contrast between the seasons or a very short growing season, you might have to help your plants along by starting them inside for four to six weeks before transplanting them outside, or moving them inside during cold nights and putting them under lights to prevent cold damage.

PICKING YOUR STRAIN

Once you've looked into the grow environment, you're ready to pick a strain (or multiple strains). With outdoor growing, your choice of strains can make all the difference between a nice harvest and a busted season. Here are a few tips to guide you along the way:

- Good genetics are key to a good grow: Buy the best seeds you can afford.

- If your growing season is very short, consider buying an auto-flowering strain (a strain that has been crossed with *C. ruderalis* parents).

- As discussed, if you live in a hot, wet climate, consider a tropical *sativa*.

- Look online for grow journals on your favorite strains: Many growers post detailed notes about their experiences with certain strains.

- Talk to a seed bank about which seeds will do best in your environment.

PRO TIP: STAGGER YOUR HARVEST

By picking a few strains with different flowering times, you can stagger your outdoor harvest. This not only spreads out the work of harvesting, but also ensures a steady supply of fresh buds. This is possible even if you're only growing two plants!

STARTING YOUR OUTDOOR GROW

Outdoor growing can be as simple as sowing seeds directly into the soil, much like corn or wheat fields are sown. However, this isn't recommended. High-quality marijuana seeds can be expensive, and the failure rate of young plants grown this way is high. Instead, you should start your plants indoors and move them outside when they're ready for the vegetative stage (instructions provided in Chapter 2).

It's also recommended that you start your plants and prepare your outdoor growing site simultaneously. This way, your location will be ready when it's time to transplant the seedlings or clones. If it's too early in the season to work your soil because it's still frozen, don't worry: Your plants will be inside for around one month before you can transplant, so you will have plenty of time to improve your patch while your seedlings are still growing and the ground is thawed.

STARTING YOUR PLANTS

You can use either seedlings or clones for your outside grow. If you're using seedlings, make sure to add between one and six weeks to your overall grow cycle to account for the germination and seedling stages. If you're using clones, they will be further along and may only need two weeks indoors before you can start the process of moving them outside. In either case, the key to knowing when it's safe to begin the transplant process is by looking at your plant's roots. Your young plant should have a nice root structure, with visible white roots in the soil ball. To check this, you can gently remove the plant from its container. Your plant should also be putting out mature leaves and growing vigorously. In either approach (seedlings or clones), the following tips will help you as you start your plants:

- Start indoors, under either a florescent or LED light. You can use a standard LED or florescent grow light at this stage.

- Put a fan on the plants early, to help them develop strong stems (you'll want to support them with bamboo stakes beforehand).

- Start with an 18/6 photoperiod instead of a 24-hour photoperiod so you don't accidentally send the plants into flowering when you move them outside, especially if you're planting earlier in the season when the photoperiod is still shorter.

With this advice in mind, you'll follow the same process outlined in Chapter 2 for starting your seedlings and clones.

WHY THE BAD REP?

Many people assume that indoor marijuana is superior to outdoor marijuana. There are a few reasons for this, including the fact that most of the manicured, bright green buds featured in professional photographs are indoor plants. But there's likely another reason at work. Indoor growing is a much newer method than outdoor growing; it's only been possible at this level of ease since the late 1990s. Before that, marijuana was exclusively grown outside. And due to the laws surrounding marijuana, those growing the plant in the US before modern indoor growing advancements often had to choose suboptimal spots, harvest too early, and rush the drying and curing of their buds. Today, outdoor growers are able to dedicate more time and resources to producing high-quality outdoor marijuana.

PREPARING YOUR GROW SITE

Take advantage of the time your plants are indoors to prepare your grow site. Ideally, you'll be planting as temperatures are warming up after the colder months (typically in March or April if you are growing in the US), but this will of course depend on climate variations and when your soil has thawed. Marijuana is a surprisingly cold-hardy plant, but you still don't want to plant when the nights are regularly below 50°F, as marijuana growth is seriously slowed or even stops below this temperature.

AMENDING THE SOIL

Unless you are fortunate enough to live in an area with rich, dark soil, you'll also want to improve your soil with something called a "soil amendment." A soil amendment is any material you mix into the soil to improve its physical or chemical properties. Your exact soil-improvement regimen will depend on your soil type, but the following are some common soil amendments. For instructions on how to add the amendment to your soil and in what amount, do your research first (paying particular attention to safety issues), and always refer to the amendment packaging:

- **Peat moss.** Also known as "sphagnum moss," peat moss is harvested from peat bogs. This has been a very popular soil amendment for years, thanks to its excellent water retention and drainage properties. However, environmentally conscious growers are encouraged not to use it, as peat is not a sustainable resource, and the world's peat bogs are under stress. Additionally, peat rapidly decomposes and lowers the pH of your soil, so you typically need to add dolomite lime (an alkaline base) to the amendment to offset this (unless you have soil with a high concentration of lime: In this case, the peat will help lower the pH toward a friendlier zone).

- **Compost.** Compost is sometimes called "black gold" because of its value in the garden and its environmental benefits. It is a mixture of organic, often decaying, material that is either neutral in pH or slightly alkaline, and provides nutrients and beneficial microorganisms for your soil. Compost can also help balance out the pH in soils that are too alkaline (such as a soil with lots of limestone) or too acidic (such as a peat-based soil).

PRO TIP: MINE FOR BLACK GOLD

Compost is one of the best soil amendments available—and it's free! If you don't already compost, consider trying it out. Outdoor compost bins are widely available, and there are hundreds of resources on how to get started. If you have yard space, you can create a compost pile outside. Indoor composting is also available, thanks to specialized devices that reduce smell and can handle food and kitchen scraps. In addition to being an ideal soil amendment, composting reduces the amount of waste you're putting into your garbage bins and provides lasting benefit to your soil.

- **Manure.** Manure is an excellent soil amendment, either produced from your own animals or purchased from a garden store or online. Be aware, however, that manure is heavy and dense, and has poor aeration, so you'll need to use something like mulch to improve your soil's drainage.

- **Perlite and vermiculite.** These are not typically used to improve outdoor soil, but if you're growing in an area with dense clay soil in which you have to dig out planting holes and backfill with a soil mix, you might need to add either of these to your planting hole.

- **Coconut coir.** Available in bales, this is a much better option than peat moss. As a renewable resource, coconut coir is more environmentally responsible and has a naturally slightly acidic pH, which marijuana likes. Coir also has excellent water retention capacity, good drainage, and the ability to resist compaction better than peat. Before planting, however, it's important to rinse your coir as well as possible (you can do this in the planting hole if necessary, flushing with copious water before adding other amendments); coir is often harvested from seaside coconut farms and may have a high sodium level. This can interfere with the uptake of calcium and magnesium into the plant roots if unrinsed.

In addition to these main soil amendments, you might want to add some more specialized amendments for extra nutrients. These are often called "minor amendments," since they don't change the structure of the soil. A little planning here will go a long way: Some of these minor amendments need time to break down in the soil before they become available to your plant, so even one week can make a difference. Do some research first, and follow package instructions for proper dosing and more details on specific minor amendments (including pet safety). Common minor amendments include:

- **Bone meal.** This is a great way to add extra calcium and phosphorus to your soil. Bone meal is an important amendment in organic gardens and safe to use with any plant you're going to consume (be sure to buy a US-made bone meal). Bone meal is slow to break down, so will provide a steady supply of nutrients throughout the growing season.

- **Blood meal.** Blood meal is high in nitrogen, which your marijuana will use to produce lush leaves and vegetative growth. Like bone meal, this soil amendment is also popular in organic gardens (be sure to buy a US-made blood meal). It breaks down quickly.

- **Dolomite lime.** If you're growing in an acidic soil, dolomite lime can be used to bring your pH up to a friendlier range.

BUILDING RAISED BEDS

If you're dealing with a very heavy clay soil, or you have the room and access for it, a raised planting bed is a great way to grow marijuana outdoors. While you can purchase raised planting beds online or in garden stores, you can also make your own at home from regular lumber, corrugated metal, or many other construction materials. If you're using wood, avoid pressure-treated lumber (like deck lumber) or railroad ties, as these materials have been treated with chemicals that you don't want leaching into your soil. Instead, use a long-lasting hardwood like red cedar. Although these are more expensive, they are naturally beautiful and will last for years. You can also use cement blocks, but be aware that cement will gradually leach concrete into the soil, raising your soil pH (concrete is alkaline). Over time, you will have to amend your soil to bring the pH back toward neutral.

To build a raised planting bed:

1 Measure your space and cut your lumber to fit. In general, you need a raised bed that is at least 12" deep to allow for healthy root growth.

2 If you are making a wooden bed, drive one 4" × 4" wooden pole into the ground at each of the four corners of where the bed will be. The pole should extend above ground to the height of your planting bed, with another 18" or so buried underground.

3 Attach your side boards to the poles to form the bed, making the boards as snug as possible.

4 Turn the existing soil over, or cover it with landscape fabric (this depends on the quality of your underlying soil).

5 Fill the bed with your soil mix.

PRO TIP: GROW IN OUTDOOR CONTAINERS

If you don't have room to grow in the ground, or if you have poor soil, growing outdoor marijuana in containers is an excellent option. This gives you total control over the type of soil you're using so you can provide optimum conditions. Container-based growing outside isn't much different than container-based growing indoors—with a few exceptions. First, you'll want a bigger container, up to 25 gallons. Also make sure that your container is heavy enough to withstand the elements.

TRANSPLANTING

Transplanting is a big day for your young plants: They will be making the jump from their small containers and indoor/outdoor environment to a permanent outdoor environment. Don't be surprised if it takes your plants a few days to acclimate after transplantation. As mentioned in Chapter 2, transplanting involves some shock no matter how careful you are; you might see a pause in new growth for a week or so, followed by an explosion of growth as the plant adjusts to its sunny outdoor home.

While Chapter 2 discusses transplanting in more detail, the following are key things to keep in mind as you transplant your marijuana plants:

- Have your grow site completely prepared before transplanting —this might include digging planting holes and filling with improved soil, building raised beds, or turning over and improving a patch of soil.

- Ensure your plants are hardened off.

- Water the soil so it's moist, but not soggy.

- Plant your marijuana so the top of the root ball is level with the soil.

- Water thoroughly after you plant.

- Stake up the plants if strong winds are an issue.

- Install any prepurchased or designed security fences to keep out rabbits, deer, and other critters.

Once your plants are in the ground, you'll want to visit them as often as possible. This will give you a chance to water them, check for pests and bugs, and ensure they are developing strong stems.

PRO TIP: USE FIBER POTS TO REDUCE SHOCK

If you're planning on growing outdoors, consider using fiber pots for your seedlings or clones. These pots are made from a biodegradable fiber that you can plant directly into the ground without disturbing the plants. Instead of removing your plants from their pots during transplant, you simply tear off the bottom of the container and plant it whole (using the cutaway method described in Chapter 2). The marijuana roots will grow out of the bottom of the container and eventually through the sides.

MULCHING

Mulch is a gardener's best friend, so consider applying mulch to your marijuana planting area when you plant. In a forest, mulch is naturally created from decaying forest products, but you'll most likely buy it in bags from a local garden store or online. Mulch has many benefits for your marijuana grow, including:

- Preserving moisture in the soil
- Preventing weeds from invading your growing area
- Providing additional nutrients as it breaks down
- Encouraging growth of beneficial bacteria and microorganisms

When applying mulch, aim for a 4" layer on your planting area. Don't push the mulch up around the base of your plants. Once you've spread it, water the mulch lightly so it is moist but not soggy. This will help "lock" the mulch into position.

GROWING ORGANIC MARIJUANA

At the most basic level, organic gardening means growing your plants without the use of synthetic fertilizers and pesticides. In practice, organic gardening is often an overall approach to growing things that seeks to promote a healthy balance of life in your growing area. Organic gardeners work to naturally improve the soil to create a healthy ecosystem for their plants. This especially makes sense with marijuana because you'll be consuming the result of your labor; it's common sense that you wouldn't put something on or in your plants that you wouldn't put in your body. Overall, it's recommended that you grow organically whenever possible. It's good for the environment, plus many people swear organic marijuana tastes better.

Some of the basic principles of organic gardening include:

1 **Improving your soil naturally.** Soil is the basis of all gardening, and healthy soil should be rich with organic material and beneficial bacteria, fungi, and other microorganisms. The soil amendments outlined previously in this chapter are all natural improvements.

2 **Working with nature, not against it.** This means preventing problems before they occur through a smart garden design. An organic garden is a balanced system with a reduced vulnerability to insects and invasive weeds.

3 **Starting with the least toxic solution.** It's a misconception that organic gardeners don't use any chemicals. They do when

necessary; however, they start with the least harmful solution first. If you must use chemicals, only use those that are approved for organic gardening. You can find information about approved organic gardening products online.

The approaches to outdoor marijuana growing that have been explored in this chapter are all in line with these principles.

Organic fertilizers for marijuana include:

- Compost tea and compost (covered in Chapter 6)
- Earthworm castings (covered in Chapter 6)
- Bat guano (covered in Chapter 6)
- Fish and seaweed emulsions (covered in Chapter 6)

Organic pest control solutions include:

- Neem oil
- Garlic
- Cayenne pepper
- Horticultural oil
- Pyrethrum

The main organic pest control solutions (neem oil, garlic, horticultural oil, and pyrethrum) will be covered in greater depth in Chapter 9, but a quick word on pyrethrum: Pyrethrum is a common organic pesticide derived from the extract of a certain kind of chrysanthemum flower. It is a broad-spectrum insecticide that's effective against a wide variety of insects, including aphids and other pests. Although pyrethrum is approved for organic gardening, it should be your last resort. Also note that pyrethrum-derived products should be distinguished from pyrethroids. Pyrethroids are synthetic pesticides that should not be used on marijuana plants under any circumstances.

DEALING WITH CHALLENGES

When you're growing marijuana in the great outdoors, you will inevitably come across a few challenges. Some of the obvious issues are related to climate—for example, a drought might hit your area that season, or torrential autumn rains could damage your developing flowers. And of course, there are many pests that might find your marijuana as delightful as you do.

The first and best thing you can do is to plan your garden with these challenges in mind. This means finding a good, open spot that's protected and has privacy. Some growers locate their crops in the middle of brambles or other spiny plants to discourage unwanted visitors. Other growers use fencing to keep marijuana-loving animals like deer out of their crops. Some of these challenges will be discussed in more detail in Chapter 9, but you'll find an overview of common issues and how to plan for them in the following sections.

SHORT GROWING SEASONS

Short growing seasons are typical of northern latitudes, where the colder months leave grudgingly and come back early. They are also typical of alpine regions, where temperatures are cooler and the air is drier. If you are faced with a short growing season due to your grow location, the solution is twofold. First, pick your genetics carefully to find a cold-hardy strain that flowers quickly. Autoflowering strains are a good fit in this situation, and many popular strains have been introduced as autoflowering plants. Second, you can extend your growing season by starting your plants indoors or, if you have the room and resources, by growing your plants in an outdoor greenhouse or hoop house.

⚝ WHAT ARE AUTOFLOWERING STRAINS?

Strains that are identified as autoflowering have been crossed with *C. ruderalis* parents. Unlike *C. sativa*, the *ruderalis* plant flowers based on its age, not on the light cycle. By introducing *C. ruderalis* genes, breeders have created marijuana plants that flower after a certain number of weeks and don't depend on changing light cycles. Although autoflowering strains are reported to have less THC, they are a good option for a beginning grower because they flower fast (some strains can go from seed to harvest in eight weeks) and you can keep your lights set on an 18/6 cycle for the entire grow.

SUBTROPICAL CONDITIONS

There are some regions (including the southeast coastal areas in the US) that experience very hot, humid seasons with a tremendous amount of rain. This is not the natural habitat for most marijuana, and you'll quickly learn that bud rot can pose a big problem in this situation. The best solution here is to pick a strain that can thrive in these conditions. A tropical *sativa* is your best option; look for strains that do well in places like Hawaii, Jamaica, or Thailand. You can also grow in either of the shoulder seasons to avoid the hotter months.

ANIMALS

Marijuana is a beloved plant to many of nature's four-legged friends. The following are the worst offenders in the US. If you live outside of the US, or want more details on the animals to watch out for in your area, check online forums and local seed banks:

- **Deer.** Deer love marijuana and can easily destroy a whole patch in one day. The best solution is a physical barrier like a fence. A good deer-proof fence has to be at least 6' tall (ideally closer to 8') to keep them from leaping over it and into your garden. If this isn't practical for your growing situation, you can take steps to try deterring them. There are many natural deer repellents on the market, which use scents from different predators to keep the deer away. (Do your research to make sure you find the safest option.)

- **Rabbits.** Rabbits are voracious consumers of all things green, including marijuana. Like with deer, the best solution is fencing. A rabbit fence should be made from wire mesh or chicken wire and buried at least 6" deep to prevent burrowing. The fence should also be at least 2' tall. If a rabbit fence isn't possible, you can also use a commercial rabbit deterrent.

PESTS

Insect pests are a common problem for outdoor gardeners, but there is some good news: Unlike indoors, where pest populations can multiply unchecked, your outdoor pests will have natural predators like wasps and spiders that should help keep them under control. Marijuana is also a robust, fast-growing plant that can withstand attacks by many insects. Your plants are most vulnerable during flowering, when the resin-heavy flowers provide a very tempting target for mites and other insects.

Insect pests will be covered in more detail in Chapter 9, but the general rule is to pay close attention to your plants to identify insect problems as early as possible, then use the least-toxic option to treat them. Sometimes you can stop a problem with a simple spray of water to blast insects off your plants. A bit of prevention and quick thinking can eliminate a lot of problems later on.

FIVE TIPS TO REMEMBER

Growing marijuana outside can be incredibly rewarding, producing huge plants that yield large amounts of high-quality bud. To maximize your chances of a successful grow, follow these five main tips from this chapter:

1   **Get to know your environment.** The main factor in your success will be knowing your particular growing environment, including typical rainfall, frost periods, and what type of soil you have to work with.

2   **Improve your soil.** Unless you're lucky enough to be growing in rich farmland, improving your soil with amendments like compost and mulch will yield better plants.

3   **Pick the right strain.** Outdoors, where your plants will be subjected to the whims of nature, it's important to pick a strain that can handle your environment. If you live in a short-season area, for example, consider an autoflowering strain. If you live in the subtropics, a *sativa*-dominant tropical strain might be perfect.

4 **Visit your plants as often as possible.** Well-tended gardens thrive! Make sure to visit your plants often and inspect them closely for signs of pests, water distress (e.g., wilting), and other problems.

5 **Anticipate problems and treat issues quickly.** If you live in an area with deer, it will be worth putting up a fence before you plant. If you see evidence of mites on your plants, move quickly to deal with them.

CHAPTER 6

Stages of Marijuana Growth:

Vegetative Growth

During the vegetative growth period, your marijuana will grow from a seedling into a mature plant, getting taller and branching out as it prepares for flowering. The principles of success in vegetative growth are the same whether you're growing inside or outside, in soil or in a hydroponic system. You'll need to provide your plants with optimum levels of light, nutrients, air, and water in order for them to thrive.

In this chapter, you'll explore these principles in more detail, learning easy strategies you can use to support healthy vegetative growth and maximize your yield. First, you'll look at the light cycle of vegetative growth. Then, you'll dive deeper into the world of fertilizer and the important nutrients for a healthy crop. Finally, you'll learn more about how to properly prune and train your plants as they grow. So, let's get started.

THE VEGETATIVE LIGHT CYCLE

As you learned earlier, usually marijuana's life cycle is determined by how much light it gets each day. When your plants were seedlings or new clones, you kept them under either 24-hour or 18-hour light. During the vegetative stage, you'll continue to provide as much light as possible. (An insufficient amount of light will lead to leggy and weak plants.) This means you'll either transplant them outside during the warmer months, when the days are growing longer, or move them into an indoor vegetative grow area and set the lights on a cycle of 18/6 (18 hours of light, 6 hours of dark each day) or 24/0 (24 hours of light each day). If you're growing indoors, do your best to make sure the dark hours are truly dark. While the lights are off, the growing area should be lightproof, or as dark as possible.

18/6 OR 24/0?

During vegetative growth indoors, you can use either an 18/6 or 24/0 light cycle—but which is better? The majority of growers use 18/6, although this is often about reducing power bills versus increasing yield. While you can find many arguments for either cycle online, as long as you're providing at least 18 hours of light during vegetative growth, you have nothing to worry about.

FERTILIZER AND PLANT NUTRITION

Horticulturists have identified eighteen elements that plants require to survive. The first three are carbon, hydrogen, and oxygen. These are naturally present in the environment, or are provided through watering. The remaining fifteen need to be provided in the growing environment and can be broken down into three broad categories:

1 **Primary macronutrients.** These are the main nutrients plants need. A deficiency in any of the macronutrients will affect your plant's growth, resulting in poor performance or even death. The primary macronutrients include:

   - Nitrogen
   - Phosphorus
   - Potassium

2 **Secondary macronutrients.** These nutrients are also used in large quantities, but are less vital to a plant's survival. The nutrients in this group include:

   - Calcium
   - Magnesium
   - Sulfur

3 **Micronutrients.** These essential elements are used in much smaller quantities than macronutrients and secondary macronutrients. The list of micronutrients includes:

   - Iron
   - Boron
   - Copper
   - Chlorine
   - Manganese
   - Molybdenum
   - Zinc
   - Cobalt
   - Nickel

These three categories of nutrients are fed to your plants via fertilizer. A complete fertilizer will have a combination of all three. The following sections give more information about primary and secondary macronutrients and the things to look for when purchasing fertilizer for your marijuana plants.

DO I NEED TO WORRY ABOUT MICRONUTRIENTS?

While experienced and professional growers have mastered the art of creating the ideal environment for marijuana, including the exact levels of micronutrients needed at every life stage, you can provide micronutrients in an easy way by buying a high-quality fertilizer complete with micronutrients, or by using an organic fertilizer. When you're buying fertilizer, just look on the label to ensure that it includes the micronutrients listed previously.

PRIMARY MACRONUTRIENTS

The three primary macronutrients listed previously form the basis of most fertilizers. When you look at a fertilizer package, you'll see them printed on the label in what is known as the "NPK ratio." An example of a balanced NPK ratio is a standard 20-20-20 fertilizer. This means the fertilizer is:

- 20 percent nitrogen (N)
- 20 percent phosphorus (P)
- 20 percent potassium (K)

A higher percentage means that fertilizer has more of that particular nutrient (measured by weight). Typically, synthetic fertilizers have higher concentrations of the primary macronutrients than organic fertilizers.

Each of the primary macronutrients plays an important role in plant growth. The following list breaks down each macronutrient and its role in helping your marijuana thrive:

- **Nitrogen (N).** Nitrogen is essential for healthy leaf and foliage growth. Plants that get plenty of nitrogen have lush, green leaves.

- **Phosphorus (P).** Phosphorus helps your plants develop healthy roots and flowers. A fertilizer with a higher phosphorus level is known as a "bloom booster" because it helps support healthier, bigger flowers.

- **Potassium (K).** Potassium is a nutrient that supports overall plant health and helps your plant produce plenty of chlorophyll (the green photosynthetic pigment in the plant's leaves).

Plants in the vegetative stage require more nitrogen, while plants in the flowering stage require more phosphorus. Your plant will also let you know if there's a deficiency in any of the primary macronutrients. The following chart lists the signs of deficiency for each macronutrient and how to correct them:

PRIMARY MACRONUTRIENT	SIGNS OF DEFICIENCY	ACTION
Nitrogen	• Slow growth • Yellow leaves • Leaves dropping off	Fertilize with a high-N fertilizer. Use a fast-acting organic fertilizer such as a high-N bat guano to boost nitrogen quickly.

Phosphorus	• Stunted growth • Smaller leaves • Irregular blotches on leaves • Delayed flowering • Smaller buds	Correct pH to 5.5–6.5 to encourage uptake of phosphorus. Use a high-P fertilizer, or a fast-acting organic high-P fertilizer.
Potassium	• Spots on leaves • Weak stems	Thoroughly flush your soil with clean water to wash out excess salt, then use a complete fertilizer.

SECONDARY MACRONUTRIENTS

While your first consideration when buying fertilizer is the NPK ratio, you should still pay attention to the secondary macronutrients of calcium, magnesium, and sulfur. Each of these plays an important role in plant health. In the following list, you will find more details about each secondary macronutrient and its role in the growth of your marijuana plants:

- **Calcium (Ca).** Just as it does with human bones, calcium plays an important role in building strong cells and structures in plants. Calcium deficiencies are rare in outdoor plants, but may occur in hydroponic gardens.

- **Magnesium (Mg).** Magnesium is involved in the process of photosynthesis.

- **Sulfur (S).** Sulfur contributes to healthy enzyme levels and other basic plant functions. Although sulfur is considered a secondary macronutrient, marijuana requires only a very small amount of sulfur, and deficiencies are extremely rare. If you're providing correct levels of calcium and magnesium, you'll likely never need to worry about sulfur.

The following chart lists the signs of secondary macronutrient deficiencies and how to correct them:

SECONDARY MACRONUTRIENT	SIGNS OF DEFICIENCY	ACTION
Calcium	• Discolored brown spots on leaves and leaf edges • Very slow growth • Stunted plants • Reduced flowering	Use lime supplements to boost calcium levels quickly. Bone meal breaks down slowly and should only be used as a supplement in the beginning of your grow.
Magnesium	• Brown and curled up leaf tips, which eventually fall off	Use a solution of Epsom salts (magnesium sulfate) at 1 tablespoon per gallon of water.
Sulfur	• Leaves that turn light green and progress to yellow, then fall off	Use a liquid fertilizer with adequate sulfur.

TIPS FOR USING FERTILIZER

When you're shopping for fertilizer, it can seem like there is a dizzying array of options. But don't worry: As long as you're providing a high-quality, balanced product at the right time (vegetative growth versus flowering), your plants will thrive! Of course, you will also need to know how to feed the fertilizer to your plants. While fertilizer will allow your marijuana to grow to its full potential, too much of it can be toxic, damaging your plants. Here are simple tips for using fertilizer correctly:

1 Think about how you are going to feed your plants before you plant them. Your growing medium and location will inform the fertilizer you need.

2 Always follow label instructions on your chosen fertilizer. Do your research for any precautions for you or your plants.

3 Use organic products whenever possible (more on this later in this chapter).

4 Although slow-release fertilizers are wonderful products, they aren't ideal for marijuana cultivation. Marijuana tends to have a short life cycle, and these products break down too slowly for the plants to use all of their great nutrients.

5 It's better to provide a steady, smaller supply of weak fertilizer than a larger dose of strong fertilizer.

6 Not all strains have the same nutrient requirements. Look online for information about what type of fertilizer and fertilizer strength will work best for your chosen strain.

7 Plants in the vegetative state require a fertilizer with a higher nitrogen level (N) to encourage strong leaf growth. As your plants

transition into the flowering stage, however, switch to a fertilizer that provides a higher level of phosphorus (P) to encourage bigger buds. (Flowering will be covered in more detail in Chapter 7.)

ORGANIC FERTILIZER

Growing organic marijuana is recommended whenever possible. After all, it's going to be consumed, so it's important to reduce the use of chemicals during your grow. To this end, it's helpful to understand what makes an organic fertilizer different from a non-organic fertilizer.

Put simply, an organic fertilizer is derived from natural sources, rather than synthesized from man-made sources. Organic fertilizers also tend to be less strong than synthetic fertilizers, and are slower to break down. In addition, organic fertilizers often contain other beneficial ingredients, including micronutrients and soil-enhancing organisms that will contribute to a healthier plant.

⟩ HOW DOES ORGANIC GROWING COMPARE?: INDOORS VERSUS OUTDOORS

When it comes to organic gardening, outdoor growers have the advantage of Mother Nature. Outside, it's possible to slowly improve a soil patch and work in harmony with your ecosystem to create a great organic growing environment. It's also easier to work outside with soil amendments that might smell too strong to use inside, like manure and some types of compost. Indoor growers, on the other hand, typically use bagged soil that lasts for only one grow, and have to supply all of the important nutrients to their plants through fertilizer. The good news is that there are many high-quality organic fertilizers available, even if you're growing hydroponically.

Common Organic Fertilizers

If you're interested in growing organically, you'll quickly discover there's a wide selection of excellent organic fertilizers available. In general, if you select an organic fertilizer from a reputable brand, you will be getting a solid product you can rely on. FoxFarm, for example, has been selling a popular line of organic fertilizers for years that are formulated to support your plants at different stages of their life cycle. If you'd like to experiment with different organic fertilizers, here are some of the most popular types:

- **Bat guano.** Bat guano is mined from caves where bats live. It's an excellent source of nitrogen for healthy vegetative growth, but you can also find guanos that are good for flowering. You can mix the powdered guano straight into your soil, or use it to make a weak compost tea (follow the directions carefully). When working with bat guano, wear protection on your hands and face and avoid breathing it in.

- **Blood meal.** Blood meal as a high-nitrogen soil supplement is covered in Chapter 5 on outdoor growing, but you can use it as a supplement for any soil-grown marijuana plant—indoors or out. Mix it directly into the soil. Be sure to buy a US-made blood meal, and keep pets away from your containers as blood meal can be toxic to animals.

- **Bone meal.** Bone meal is a high-calcium supplement that also provides phosphorus and nitrogen. Bone meal breaks down more slowly than blood meal, so it's best to amend your soil with it in the beginning of your grow. No matter your grow location, be sure to buy a US-made bone meal and be careful that pets do not have access to your plants, as bone meal can be toxic to animals.

- **Dolomite lime.** Dolomite lime is a great source of calcium and magnesium. It's also an alkaline amendment, so it can deacidify soils that have acidic ingredients, like peat moss. Some experienced growers will regularly add a tablespoon or two to their plant containers when transplanting. When purchasing, ensure that you're getting specifically dolomite lime and not another agricultural lime product, which may be too strong.

- **Fish emulsion.** Fish emulsion is created from fish by-products. It is an excellent, highly available, and balanced organic fertilizer for your plants that can even be used on young seedlings, as it's very mild. You can buy a liquid emulsion concentrate and mix it yourself, or purchase a premixed emulsion. Be aware, however, that fish emulsion has a very strong fishy odor. And if you own pets, keep them away from your plant containers after feeding; fish meal and emulsion products can be toxic to animals.

- **Fish meal.** Produced from dried and ground fish, fish meal is an excellent source of nitrogen and micronutrients. It tends to break down more slowly than other sources of organic nitrogen, supplying your plants with a steady diet of nitrogen. Beware of the smell if you are growing indoors!

- **Manure (chicken or rabbit).** If you have access to a chicken coop or rabbit hutch, you're in luck. Manure from these animals is a wonderful organic fertilizer, with high levels of macronutrients and minor elements. Because fresh manure (especially rabbit) is hard to find in larger quantities, you can also buy dried and composted chicken manure and mix it directly into the soil.

- **Seaweed meal or emulsions.** Seaweed is high in nitrogen, trace elements, and even vitamins and hormones. You can buy a fast-acting liquid seaweed fertilizer or a seaweed meal. Read up on it first, and look into different brands before purchasing, as high salt levels in some seaweed meal or emulsion fertilizers can be toxic to your plants.

- **Worm castings.** Worm castings are remains of soil products excreted by worms. Worm castings are a great source of nitrogen and other trace elements. You can use worm castings as a direct soil amendment, mixing it into your soil as you prepare to transplant. It's impossible to burn your plants with worm castings, although they can be heavy and reduce drainage, so make sure to add plenty of drainage-enhancing ingredients like perlite if you're using worm castings.

PRO TIP: MAKE IT A TEA

As you grow in your confidence with organic fertilizers, you might try making compost or fertilizer teas for your plants. Just like drinking tea, a compost or fertilizer tea is made by steeping ingredients in water, then using that water to feed your plants. There are many ways to mix up an organic compost tea, so it's worth doing a little research if you'd like to try it. Teas provide a readily available source of nutrients, because the nutrients are already suspended in a water solution. They are also very gentle—it's virtually impossible to burn your plants with a compost or nutrient tea.

PRUNING MARIJUANA

Once you have the feeding element of your marijuana's vegetative growth down, it's time to look into pruning. If you let your marijuana grow naturally, without trimming or training any branches, it will grow into a Christmas tree–shaped plant, with large fan leaves near the bottom, side branches, and a main growing point at the top. Marijuana typically blooms from the top down, so the flower that forms around the main stem at the top (called the "cola") will be the heaviest.

Depending on your grow location, it might be fine to leave your marijuana untouched throughout its life so it can grow into its natural shape and size. This is especially true for outdoor growers, where untrimmed marijuana can get huge and yield a pound or more of bud per plant, with multiple colas growing on large branches. However, for many growers, some pruning and shaping is necessary. For example, indoor growers often prune and shape their plants to reduce competition for available light and encourage their plants to bloom in a specific way for the maximum yield.

Before diving into the different pruning techniques, it's helpful to understand how the marijuana plant grows and flowers. From the time your marijuana plant enters vegetative growth, it will put out branches that grow perpendicular to the main stem. At each point that a pair of leaves emerges from a branch or the stem, there is a node. Nodes are biologically important areas: This is where the flowers will form. The more nodes you have, the more flowers your plant will form, and thus the more buds you can harvest.

When you're pruning marijuana, the goal is to maximize the plant's flowering potential. This might mean increasing the number of flowering nodes, or it might mean severely limiting the number of flowering nodes. If you're growing few plants with abundant light, then the more nodes you have, the better. Your plants will respond by producing heavy harvests. However, if you're packing more plants in a smaller space, you'll limit the number of nodes on each plant so individual plants put their energy into producing one or two large buds and don't shade out their neighbors.

HOW TO PRUNE YOUR MARIJUANA

With this information in mind, you can create a pruning strategy that best fits your unique growing conditions. To prune your marijuana once your strategy is established, simply follow these easy steps:

1 Identify the branches you want to remove.

2 Using a sharp, sterile instrument such as pruning shears, a razor, or a pair of kitchen scissors, cut the branches at a 45-degree angle. (Never use outdoor pruners on indoor plants: You could be transferring pests or diseases into your growing space.)

After you prune a branch, your plant will put out two smaller branches from the nearest node. Each of these new branches will have additional flowering sites. While this sounds like a great idea, it is very possible to overprune marijuana. Your plant's maximum number of flowering sites is genetically predetermined. At some point, you can't improve the plant's yield and you'll only be damaging the plant. This will be different for every strain, so it'll take some practice to master, but it's always a good idea to prune conservatively at first. You can also find pruning details and tips for specific strains online.

⇝ WHAT ABOUT THE LARGE LOWER FAN LEAVES?

For a long time, marijuana growers were advised to remove large lower fan leaves as the plant neared flowering. The thought was that removing these leaves allowed the plant to put more energy into developing big buds. An extreme version of this, where almost all of the fan leaves are removed, is known as the schwazzing technique. Today, however, there's more debate around this practice. Remember: Fan leaves are the growth engines that power your plant. So, consider leaving the big fan leaves on your plants. If one is shading a developing flowering site, you can simply tuck it back out of the way. If you must remove fan leaves, focus on yellowing or old leaves.

TOPPING YOUR MARIJUANA

"Topping" is a type of pruning that is performed only on the top growing node, where the cola would form. Topping plants is a common gardening technique to limit plant size and increase yield—and marijuana is no different. When you top a marijuana plant, the main branch will split into two branches. Each of these branches can form a cola. In some cases, you can top your plants twice, resulting in four colas on each plant. (See Figure 6.1.)

Topping should always be done during vegetative growth. Typically, you would top a plant between the fourth and sixth nodes. Once your plant has begun to develop calyx, it's too late to top. To top your marijuana, simply locate the main growing stem and snip off the very top set of leaves below the growing node.

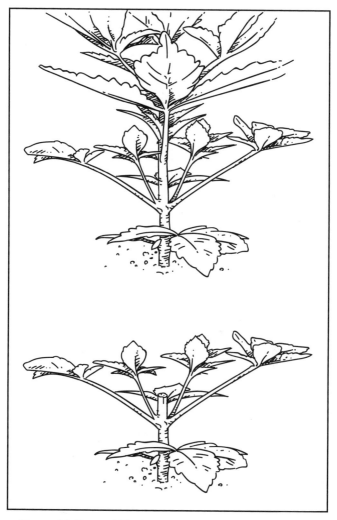

▲ Figure 6.1: Topped Plant

→ WHAT IS THE DIFFERENCE BETWEEN THINNING AND PRUNING?

Pruning your marijuana plant is not the same thing as thinning it. In horticulture, thinning generally means to physically remove plants from the growing space, usually by cutting them down. This is done to increase the available amount of growing space for each plant. In marijuana cultivation, you'd only thin your plants early on, to remove spindly seedlings. You might also thin your plants during preflowering to remove males. Otherwise, you'll focus on pruning, which is the selective removal of branches or plant parts to get a desired effect.

TRAINING MARIJUANA

Training marijuana is another popular approach growers use to increase their yields and maximize their growing space. You might also want to train your plants to keep them from overgrowing fences or getting too close to your lights. Training marijuana involves the same principles used in bonsai gardening: the application of pressure over time to force your plant to grow in the direction you want. This is often called "low-stress training," or LST, because there is no cutting and little stress put on the plant itself. (See Figure 6.2.) When combined with careful pruning, you'll quickly learn that training your marijuana allows you to grow it successfully in almost any situation. You can even get that heady *sativa* to thrive in a small space.

▴ Figure 6.2: Low-Stress Training

Since your plants have a genetically predetermined maximum number of flowering nodes, it might take some experience with the same strain to figure out how much training they can withstand. It's recommended that you start with the most basic training at first until you get a feel for it.

To train your marijuana, follow these easy steps:

1 When your plant is young and still supple, before the stem has become woody, attach a wire or string to the stem about

two-thirds of the way up the plant. This is best done early in the vegetative growth stage.

2 Using the wire or string, gently pull on the plant, causing it to bend over. You can start training the day you tie the plant down and gradually increase how far you're bending branches. If the plant is young enough, you can bend it into the desired shape on the first day.

3 Attach the wire or string to the edge of the container through holes, or to a stake or other wire.

As you're training your plants, you'll see them immediately respond. The leaves will quickly turn to face the light, and the growing tip on the main stem will also turn up, forming an *S* shape. As new branches come in, they will also grow upward, effectively forming a row of small mini-colas. If you'd like to limit your plant's horizontal growth, you would combine training with topping and snip off the main growing node.

PRO TIP: DON'T GIRDLE YOUR MARIJUANA

When you're staking up and training your marijuana, you will be working with string (or monofilament line or twine). Be careful not to actually loop the string around your marijuana stem so it encircles the stem completely. The risk is that your marijuana will grow too large for the string, which will cut into the stem and possibly even strangle the plant. This is called "girdling." To prevent this, only loop the string around your marijuana once and fasten both ends to the stake or side of the container. You can also use regular wire bent into an open hook, or even bonsai training wire.

HEADING TOWARD HARVEST

Vegetative growth will likely be the easiest part of your grow to manage. During this time, you will focus on two main jobs: feeding your plants for maximum growth (focusing on a high-nitrogen fertilizer and supplying all the macronutrients and micronutrients your plants need) and preparing for maximum flowering. It's important to note, however, that there isn't one "right" approach to vegetative growth that suits every situation. In fact, your ideal vegetative growth strategy will be highly dependent on how you're growing your marijuana. If you're growing inside, you will likely be more concerned with pruning and getting the fertilizer schedule right than if you're growing outside. If you're growing outside in a well-prepared, fertile bed, you'll be more concerned with fending off pests and other problems (see Chapters 5 and 9) and may not need to prune at all.

Whatever your approach is, the end of vegetative growth marks a change in your grow: You'll finally be heading toward the harvest you've been working toward all this time. The next chapter will discuss flowering, and give you tips on how to ensure you have the biggest harvest of high-potency marijuana possible.

FIVE TIPS TO REMEMBER

Success during the vegetative period is a matter of discipline and paying attention. While your plants are growing, you should be checking on them as often as possible and using the following main tips from this chapter to ensure a thriving crop:

1 **Fertilize your growing plants.** Marijuana is a hungry plant that requires ample fertilizer to perform well. During this period, focus on a high-nitrogen fertilizer with micronutrients.

2 **Pay close attention.** In addition to inspecting for pests and disease, you should also keep a close eye out for nutrient deficiencies and correct them as needed.

3 **Prune your plants as needed.** Pruning involves removing select marijuana branches to encourage better flowering. How, and if, you prune depends on your growing situation.

4 **Train your plants as needed.** Training involves "shaping" your marijuana by gently bending branches to grow in the way you want. Combined with selective pruning, this makes it possible to grow marijuana in almost any space.

5 **Watch your photoperiod.** Remember that marijuana flowers based on the photoperiod. If your indoor plants start getting less than 18 hours of sunlight daily, they may go into flowering. Outdoors, your plants will start to flower when the days become shorter. Once flowering starts, you'll switch your approach to get the biggest harvest.

CHAPTER 7

Stages of Marijuana Growth:

Flowering

Flowering is the final stage in your marijuana plant's life cycle before harvest. This is when you'll see all of your efforts paying off. It's also a time of vigilance; as you head into the flowering stage, you can expect to spend more time with your plants.

This chapter is here to help guide you through this last stage. Here, you'll first learn how to identify male and female plants during preflowering, as well as the unique purposes of each. Then, you'll explore the different aspects of flowering, as well as the main obstacles that can arise during this stage, such as fungi—and how to prevent or eliminate them. Armed with the information and tips in this chapter, you will be able to bring your marijuana plants successfully through the flowering stage and toward that highly anticipated harvest.

FLOWERING 101

Technically, the "bud" of marijuana is the dried and cured flowers of the female plant. Except for autoflowering strains, flowering is stimulated by changing light cycles. In nature, flowering corresponds to the cooler, shorter days that follow those long, hot days of vegetative growth. Indoors, flowering is triggered by changing the light cycle manually, usually shifting from a cycle of 24/0 (light for 24 hours each day) or 18/6 (light for 18 hours and dark for 6 hours each day) to 12/12 (light for 12 hours and dark for 12 hours each day). After you switch the light cycle indoors, your plants will transition from the preflowering stage to the flowering stage. Typically, full flowering begins in about two weeks.

Flowering is possible once the plant has reached sexually maturity, typically after four to six weeks of vegetative growth, or when the plant is six to eight weeks old. At this point, your plants may begin to form calyxes at the nodes, although they will likely be too small to see without a magnifying glass. Once your plants have reached sexual maturity, they can be forced into flowering by changing the light cycle at any time.

The important parts of the preflowering and flowering marijuana plant are:

- **Calyx.** This is a very early flowering structure that forms at the plant's nodes. When they first emerge, they may be very small and impossible to see with the naked eye. Over time, the calyx will grow and become recognizable as male or female preflowers.

- **Node.** This is the intersection where the stem meets the branch, where the calyx will form as the plant matures.

- **Pistil.** This is the sex organ of a female plant. On marijuana plants, pistils look like fuzzy white hairs. Pistils can emerge at any time from individual calyxes, but will develop quickly once the plant begins to flower in earnest.

- **Stipule.** A tiny hairlike structure that emerges from the node, near the calyx. (Not be confused with preflowers.)

HOW FLOWERING AFFECTS YOUR PLANTS

Just like any living thing, when your plant approaches maturity and moves through its reproductive life cycle, it will undergo certain changes. Understanding these changes will help you discern what your own plants need as they flower:

- **Stems elongate.** This is often referred to as "stretching," and it happens right at the beginning of flowering. The exact amount your plant will stretch depends on the strain, but it can grow to 100 percent or more of its preflowering height. A common indoor growing mistake for beginners is to flower the plants too late, so they stretch right into their lights and burn the buds.

- **Leaf production slows.** During flowering, your plant will still put out new leaves, but they will be smaller, with fewer blades on each leaf. This means no more big fan leaves, which is why it's recommended that you don't remove the fan leaves before flowering.

- **Cannabinoid production increases.** As the plant flowers, it will begin rapid cannabinoid production, including CBD and THC. The exact amount of cannabinoid production depends on the strain and how well it's grown. All plants have a genetically predetermined maximum for how much THC or CBD they can produce, even under perfect circumstances.

- **Nitrogen uptake slows.** As your plant shifts from focusing on producing leaves to producing flowers, it will need less nitrogen.

- **Phosphorus uptake increases.** At the same time nitrogen requirements are dropping, the plant needs extra phosphorus to produce big flowers. This means changing your fertilizer to a "bloom booster."

MALE AND FEMALE FLOWERING VARIATIONS

As discussed in Chapter 1, a marijuana plant is either male or female (if not a hermaphrodite). Without any thinning or intervention, male plants will go into flower first (one to two weeks before females). About ten days after blooming, the male flowers will open up to release pollen. If a flowering female is present, that pollen will attach to the female's sticky, resin-covered flowers and travel down into the flower to fertilize it. Once fertilized, the female plant will put its energy into seed production, eventually producing heavy cones of seeds that will carry on the next generation. The resulting offspring will inherit 50 percent of each parent plant's genetics.

PRO TIP: WATCH OUT FOR ROGUE POLLEN

Marijuana pollen is very mobile; it's easily dispersed by wind after the pollen sacs on male flowers open. In some regions where outdoor growing is popular, there's so much pollen floating around in the cooler months, often from wild-seeded marijuana, that it's hard to protect females from getting pollinated. Under the right circumstances, pollen can travel for miles.

As a grower, your goal is to prevent pollination. Instead, you are aiming to raise unfertilized female plants by protecting them from pollen, whether that means destroying male plants or setting up barriers outside to prevent rogue pollen from finding your flowering females. Why don't you want your plants to be fertilized? Because once a female is fertilized, cannabinoid production in the developing flowers drops dramatically. The plant will instead put all of its available energy into making seeds. As a result, you'll end up with a lot of seeds and fewer, less potent buds of usable marijuana.

IDENTIFYING SEX

Fortunately, with just a simple magnifying glass or photographer's 10× or 20× loupe, you can often identify and remove males before flowering begins. The process of identifying male and female plants is often referred to as "sexing." It is possible to sex plants very early, shortly after calyxes emerge during vegetative growth (usually around week four). (See Figure 7.1.) However, this can lead to misidentification, as the preflowers at this point are very small and may not be easily recognizable as male or female. Instead, it's recommended that you wait until the light cycle shifts and the plant enters the preflowering stage, which will last one to two weeks before full flowering begins. At this time, sex will become obvious and you'll have plenty of time to remove males before they go into full flower.

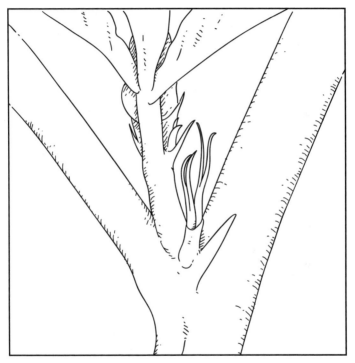

▲ Figure 7.1: Early Female Declaration

To sex a plant, you'll start at the top of the plant and look closely at the nodes with your magnifying glass or photographer's loupe. If you don't see any of the following identifiers at the top of the plant, you'll then move downward, inspecting nodes all the way down the main stem. You can also look at the nodes along the branches, moving from the branch tip toward the main stem.

Male Preflowers

A male calyx will be slightly raised on a little stalk, like an ace of spades. Eventually these spade-like preflowers will develop into little clusters of balls. Male preflowers lack the fuzzy white pistils that distinguish a female preflower. (See Figure 7.2.)

Don't cull a plant until you're sure it's a male. As a beginning grower, you should wait to cut plants until distinct preflowers have emerged. You don't want to accidentally remove a female and reduce your harvest.

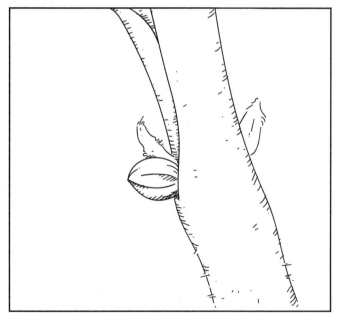

▲ Figure 7.2: Male Preflower Calyx

Female Preflowers

A female calyx will be nestled against the stem. Early on, two tiny white hairs (pistils) emerge from each calyx. They look fuzzy and may be very small. Oftentimes, the first pistils will emerge near the top of the plant, but they can come out anywhere along the stem. When the plant begins to flower, the pistils will grow and multiply in number. (See Figure 7.3.)

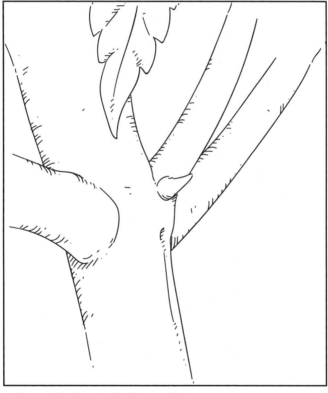

▲ Figure 7.3: Female Preflower Calyx

TRANSITIONING YOUR PLANTS INTO FLOWERING

Although triggering flowering indoors is as easy as changing your lights to a 12/12 cycle, there are a few easy things you can do to further help your plants transition into flowering, whether they are indoor or outdoor:

1 Switch to a "bloom booster" when you are ready to stimulate flowering. This fertilizer contains more phosphorus, so it will have a higher second number in its NPK ratio. Always follow package directions when adding the fertilizer to your grow.

2 Don't do any pruning or trimming for two weeks before flowering, so the plant won't be recovering from shock at the same time it is flowering.

3 If you're growing indoors, place a dehumidifier in your growing space to reduce the humidity during flowering. Keeping the humidity around 45 percent or lower will decrease the chance of a fungus attacking your flowers.

4 Mix a little molasses into your watering solution at the beginning of flowering (approximately 1 tablespoon per gallon of water every time you water). You can also purchase molasses supplements online or at a local garden store to add to your hydroponic reservoir. Molasses provides a boost of sugar to the buds and can increase their yield by as much as 20 percent.

CARING FOR YOUR PLANTS DURING FLOWERING

About two weeks after the light cycles are changed, your marijuana will begin to flower in earnest. During the first stage of flowering, the plants will experience a burst of growth, or "stretching," as discussed earlier in this chapter. While your plants are stretching, you'll want to continue feeding them with a high-quality blooming fertilizer, following the label instructions. There are also many blooming supplements on the market that claim to provide even more phosphorus and potassium. While some of these are quality products, it's recommended that beginning growers first focus on the basics, using a bloom booster that includes micronutrients (simply follow the label for dosing).

Be careful not to overfertilize. If you see any leaf tips turning brown, or spots on the leaves, you might be providing too much fertilizer, so cut back until these symptoms subside. In general, it's better to underfertilize than to damage your plants by overfertilizing.

After a few weeks of explosive stretching, flowering will slow and finally stop. Your marijuana plants have now reached their maximum flowering height. Also by this time, tiny clusters of white hairs should be growing from the nodes of your female plants and true flower structures will begin to emerge. (See Figure 7.4.)

The rate at which your buds put on weight during flowering will depend on the strain. Some strains develop heavy buds early, while others wait until the last few weeks to really pack on weight. As the female flowers get bigger, the pistils will go from white to an amber color and finally to a rust or red color. This is a sign that your flowers are maturing and producing plenty of cannabinoids. Overall, you can expect flowering to last for two to three months. However, some *sativa* and *sativa*-dominant strains will flower for twelve weeks, and some *indica* strains will flower for eight weeks.

▲ Figure 7.4: Female Flower Development

PRO TIP: DON'T OVERHANDLE THE FLOWERS

As flowering progresses, the buds of your female plants will swell with sticky resin as the plants try to attract pollen. Over time, some of these resin glands will burst, raining visible resin down onto the leaves below. Because of this, handling marijuana flowers is a sticky job and the more you handle them, the more resin sacs will burst. Try to handle your marijuana flowers as little as possible to avoid resin sacs bursting (resin is loaded with THC, so you want to preserve as much as possible!).

FUNGUS

Flowering is an exciting time for a marijuana grower—but it's also a time of vigilance. Your dense, sticky little flowers are perfect havens for fungi, as well as numerous pests that would love to share your harvest. Fungi in particular can be a real problem; whole crops can be lost quickly to spreading bud rot or gray mold (*botrytis*). Other types of fungi can attack your leaves and roots. Although fungi can attack your plants at any time, the risk increases during flowering.

IDENTIFYING FUNGUS

Especially as a beginning grower, it can feel challenging to correctly identify a problem with your plants. Fortunately, there are certain indicators in a fungal infection that can point you toward which fungus is affecting your plants. Once you've correctly identified the fungus, you can take steps to treat it.

Some of the more common types of fungi that may affect marijuana plants include:

- **Botrytis.** More commonly known as "gray mold" or "bud rot," *botrytis* targets your developing flowers, often growing deep inside the dense flowering structures. It may look like lint at first, or cause dark spots to appear on your buds. (See Figure 7.5.)

▲ Figure 7.5: Botrytis Starting

Over time, the dark spots will spread across the entire surface of the bud. (See Figure 7.6.)

▲ Figure 7.6: Full-Blown Botrytis

- **Powdery mildew.** Powdery mildew targets young leaves. It looks like a white powder on the leaves and wipes off more easily than gray mold—although this doesn't mean you've solved the problem.

- **Root rot.** This is a common problem when plants' roots are allowed to stand in water for extended periods of time. Root rot attacks these stressed roots and slowly kills them. While you can't see what's happening under the soil, you will start to see leaves turning yellow and dropping, with the plant declining from the bottom up and eventually dying.

- **Fusarium wilt.** Fusarium wilt is a familiar enemy of vegetable gardeners, but this dangerous mold doesn't stop at tomatoes and cucumbers. It's more than happy to attack your marijuana plants as well. Fusarium wilt first shows up as dry spots on leaves, followed by leaves rolling up and crisping as if they are getting burned or don't have water. Plant failure follows shortly. Fusarium spores are commonly found in soil, where they splash up onto the plant during careless watering.

If you are still uncertain of what's affecting your plants, seek out guidance from an online resource, or someone you know and trust who is a more experienced grower.

PRO TIP: CHECK OUT RODALE'S *ORGANIC GARDENER'S HANDBOOK*

There are plenty of excellent resources out there for marijuana growers, but *The Organic Gardener's Handbook of Natural Pest and Disease Control* is an all-around favorite for understanding and treating pests and disease. It lays out the principles of organic pest and disease management and is loaded with practical tips that can easily apply to your marijuana gardening.

PREVENTING FUNGUS

If you're growing outside, there's not much you can do to prevent fungi from cropping up in the grow environment. Fortunately, many types of fungi have a harder time getting established in outdoor plants than indoor plants, mostly because conditions outdoors aren't as suitable for fungi, thanks to the great airflow and copious sunshine.

If you're growing in a very humid area, however, your plants are at greater risk of fungus issues. In this case, the best defense is to pick a strain that is bred for mold resistance. Specifically, look for strains that perform well in climates like Thailand or Hawaii, where outdoor growers deal with high levels of humidity and rainfall. A few good choices include Durban Poison, Northern Lights, Power Flower, and Strawberry Cough. A local seed bank or online forum should be able to recommend other mold-resistant strains that may be a good fit for your grow.

If you're growing indoors, however, there are many easy ways to reduce the risk of fungi. These include:

- **Keeping your grow area clean.** Don't leave water sitting around or keep old growing medium in the grow area. Before you plant, wash the walls and floor with a mild bleach solution. Clean up any spills. This will be your best defense against fusarium wilt specifically.

- **Using adequate ventilation.** Fungi thrive in stagnant air. Good ventilation will help keep your growing area dry and prevent fungi from getting established.

- **Keeping the humidity around 45 percent.** Fungi thrive in high humidity. Keeping the humidity at 45 percent or lower will make it harder for fungi to get established.

- **Never bringing outdoor tools indoors.** Fungi are easily transferred on tools, so don't bring anything you've used outside into your indoor growing space.

- **Sterilizing tools between uses.** You can easily transport fungi between plants on dirty tools. Use a mild solution of isopropyl rubbing alcohol on your tools between each use.

- **Ensuring plants have good drainage and never sit in water.** This will help prevent root rot. During the vegetative phase, you may also be able to provide better drainage by transplanting.

TREATING FUNGUS

Ideally, you can prevent fungal problems by following the advice outlined in the previous section. However, even the most experienced growers may occasionally need to combat a fungal attack on their marijuana plants. The following are standard treatments for the common types of fungi, whether it attacks your plants indoors or out:

- *Botrytis*. If you see evidence of *botrytis*, time is of the essence. Snip away the affected plant material, bag it, and dispose of it. Clean your tools immediately after using them on an infected plant. Treat the remaining plant with a marijuana-safe fungicide (following the directions carefully).

- **Powdery mildew.** By the time you see powdery mildew, it's likely infected the entire plant and you'll have to treat for it. You can either remove affected plants or treat them with a marijuana-safe fungicide.

- **Root rot.** Because it affects the roots at first, root rot is identified once the plant starts to suffer. The best solution is to repot as quickly as possible and improve drainage.

- **Fusarium wilt.** Once a plant is infected with fusarium, it should be isolated and destroyed as soon as possible. This disease can't be treated with any safe fungicides.

You should also never use any strong chemical fungicides when treating fungus on your marijuana plants. These chemicals may kill the fungus, but they are unsafe to use on a marijuana plant. When it comes to treating problems like fungus (and pests), always think organic. The following are organic products commonly used to treat fungus problems like mold in marijuana:

- **Bacillus subtilis.** Bacillus subtilis (also referred to as *B. subtilis*) is actually a beneficial bacteria—much like the probiotics people take to improve their digestion. (In fact, *B. subtilis* is present in the human gut.) In marijuana cultivation, *B. subtilis* is used as a leaf spray to treat powdery mildew. The bacteria in the mixture will feed on the mildew. This product should be applied during the vegetative stage or early flowering stage.

- **Bordeaux mixture.** Bordeaux mixture is a blend of copper sulfate, lime, and water. It's an effective organic fungicide, but should only be used as a last resort in a marijuana garden because of potential health effects. Always follow label directions and don't apply on buds close to harvest time.

- **Hydrogen peroxide.** Common hydrogen peroxide is an effective and nontoxic fungicide. Use a 3 percent solution as a leaf spray and apply directly to powdery mildew or mold. You might need to repeat the treatment weekly until the fungus has been eliminated. Do not apply to buds near harvest time.

- **Neem oil.** Neem oil is derived from the neem tree and has been used in gardening (and also holistic medicine) for hundreds of years. Neem is primarily an insecticide but, when applied as a leaf spray or additive, has systemic fungicide effects as well. Neem can be applied at any time, but avoid spraying your buds near harvest.

- **Sodium bicarbonate.** Sodium bicarbonate is better known as baking soda. You can also buy horticultural preparations of sodium bicarbonate online or in garden stores. To treat mildew and mold with this method, saturate the plant (both above and under the leaves) with a mixture of 4 teaspoons of baking soda to one gallon of water. Repeat as necessary until the fungus has been eliminated. This can be used at any stage of the plant's life cycle.

- **Apple cider vinegar.** Applied at full strength, vinegar can harm marijuana, but when diluted it can act as an effective fungicide. Mix 2 teaspoons of apple cider vinegar into one quart of water and apply as a leaf spray. Repeat as necessary, until the fungus is controlled. This can be used at any stage of the plant's life cycle.

WHAT IF THE PLANT IS FURTHER ALONG IN FLOWERING?

The later in your grow that a fungus crops up, the harder it is to manage. In general, it's not a good idea to soak marijuana flowers with anything as they near maturity, and in many cases a serious fungal infection will be too deep in the flowers to reach. If a mature female plant becomes infected with a fungus near harvest, the best approach is to simply harvest the plant early and carefully cut away any infected areas. Never consume moldy buds.

THE END OF FLOWERING

When you first buy your seeds, chances are the packaging will include a general guide for how long it will take for the mature plants to finish flowering. While this is helpful information, you shouldn't rely strictly on this. Instead, it's best to keep a careful eye on your plants as they continue to pack on weight. In the next chapter, you'll learn how to tell when your plants are done flowering and it's time to harvest.

FIVE TIPS TO REMEMBER

Flowering is an exciting time, as you watch your marijuana plants pack on heavy flowers and start to look forward to harvest. Use the following main tips from this chapter to help ensure your plants successfully flower:

1 **Watch for emerging signs of male and female flowers.** During the preflowering period, your plants will show clear indicators of what sex they are and you can remove any males.

2 **Don't trim your plants during flowering or preflowering.** Trimming the plants during this time can shock your marijuana and reduce your harvest.

3 **Use a bloom-boosting fertilizer.** When your plant starts flowering (or when you switch your light cycle to 12/12 to trigger flowering) start to feed your marijuana with a bloom-boosting fertilizer. This will help encourage bigger, heavier buds.

4 **Inspect your plants carefully.** Marijuana flowers are vulnerable to pests and diseases, especially fungal infections. Pay close attention to identify problems as quickly as possible.

5 **Start with the least toxic treatment.** If you identify a pest infestation or disease, take immediate action to treat your plant—but be sure to start with the least toxic options. In some cases, for example a bad fungal infection late in flowering, it might be better to simply harvest your plant early than to attempt to treat it and lose the entire crop.

CHAPTER 8

Stages of Marijuana Growth:

Harvesting, Curing, and Manicuring

Harvest is the most exciting time for a marijuana grower—it means all of your effort and patience has paid off, and it's time to reap the rewards. Congratulations! Of course, this doesn't mean you're done: Along with harvesting, there is manicuring, drying, and curing to do, and you'll want to set aside enough time at harvest so you can do it right. After all, the difference between good bud and great bud is often this stage.

In this chapter, you'll learn the ins and outs of each stage of harvest, from determining when to harvest, to curing your harvested buds. You'll also explore the benefits of flushing your plants before harvest, so you can decide whether it is the best option for your unique growing situation. Of course, special tips and additional insights are also provided throughout the chapter, so you can navigate your harvest like a pro—even as a beginner grower.

KNOWING WHEN TO HARVEST

There are two main ways you can tell when it's time to harvest your plants: pistil color and trichomes. Each method is outlined in the following sections. No matter which method you decide to use, you'll probably notice that the changes aren't uniform throughout the plant. Many strains of marijuana ripen from the top down, so the main cola will be ready to harvest a few days before the lower buds. If you're growing a large *sativa* strain outdoors, you might harvest the plant in phases as the buds at different heights become ready. This is less common with the smaller, squatter *indica*-dominant strains.

PISTIL COLOR

Judging when to harvest based on pistil color is the old-school method, sure, but it still gives dependable results. When your female plants first go into flower, they produce white pistils. As the flower matures, those pistils begin to change color, darkening to a red, brownish, or reddish-purple color depending on the strain. When about two-thirds of the pistils on each plant have changed color, they are ready to harvest.

TRICHOMES

This is the method professional growers use, and it requires a 30× microscope. To use this method, you'll carefully inspect either the flowers or small leaves sticking out from the flowers under the microscope. Through the lens of the microscope, you'll see tiny knobbed stalks covering the surface. (See Figure 8.1.) These are called "trichomes." Trichomes contain the resin glands of the plant, where THC and other cannabinoids are produced in the highest quantity.

▲ Figure 8.1: Trichomes

As your marijuana flowers mature, their trichomes will go through three distinct phases:

1 **Clear.** These are younger trichomes that have not yet produced peak THC levels.

2 **Milky white.** These are mature trichomes that are producing higher levels of THC.

3 **Amber.** These are older trichomes that have started to decay.

You'll want to harvest when about half of the trichomes on each plant are milky and the rest are still clear. It can take a little practice to get good at telling when your trichomes are starting to change color, but even if you aren't using this method to decide when it's time to harvest, it's still a good idea to look for them. Being able to identify trichomes comes in handy when you're manicuring your bud: You can use the trimmed leaves for another purpose, such as making hash (compressed resin from a flowering plant that is smoked).

PRO TIP: USE TRICHOMES TO DETERMINE PSYCHOACTIVE EFFECTS

Once you get the hang of identifying trichomes, you can time your harvest to produce the kind of psychoactive effects you want. If you wait until the trichomes are starting to turn amber, you'll produce the "couch lock" effect (the deep body high that can make you feel "locked" into your couch) thanks to the higher production of certain cannabinoids. This is more common with *indica* plants. *Sativas* that are typically harvested when the trichomes are still 50/50 clear and milky, or even earlier, have a more energetic effect.

FLUSHING

Throughout flowering, you've been giving your plants a high-phosphorus fertilizer to support bigger, heavier buds. As your approach harvest, however, you will stop fertilizing. You might also consider "flushing" your plants before you cut them down. Flushing is the practice of running large amounts of pure water through your growing medium and switching your plants to a pure water diet, stopping any fertilizer or growth supplements. The idea is to force your plants to consume any remaining chemicals in their tissues, as well as washing out any built-up salts or minerals in the growing medium. This will improve the bud's flavor.

When you start flushing depends on the growing medium you used. For soil-based grows, you'll begin flushing one to two weeks before harvest. For a coco coir grow, you'll begin flushing one week before harvest. For a hydroponic grow, you'll begin flushing one to two days before harvest. Soil-based growers have to flush longer because soil is better at holding nutrients and minerals. Hydroponic grows can flush much more quickly because the plants are grown in a sterile medium and rely on the reservoir for nutrients.

To flush your soil-based plants or plants grown in coco coir, simply run a large quantity of clean, pure water through the growing medium. You might use five to ten times the amount of water you'd normally use when watering your plants. There will be lots of runoff, but that's the point: You're trying to wash away any impurities in the growing medium. Don't worry about over-watering: The idea is to push copious amounts of water through the growing medium, then let it drain away immediately.

To flush your hydroponic grow, simply change the reservoir to regular, pure water. After the flush, you should check the pH of your reservoir water and adjust it if necessary. Remember that hydroponic marijuana prefers a pH of 5.5–6.5.

TO FLUSH OR NOT TO FLUSH

While the concept behind flushing is simple, there is some controversy among growers as to whether it's necessary. Some growers believe that unflushed buds can have a harsh, chemical taste, while others point out that no other plants require flushing before consumption—and they don't notice any difference in taste. Ultimately, the decision is yours. You may decide to flush your first grow, then skip flushing all subsequent grows, or vice versa.

In general, hydroponic growers flush their growing medium more often than soil-based growers because they rely on more chemicals during the growing process and don't have the benefit of soil to buffer their plants. For soil-based grows, if you're following organic principles and have built a healthy soil teeming with microorganisms and organic nutrients, you can easily skip flushing without noticing any impact on your final harvest.

PRO TIP: TRY A FLUSHING PRODUCT

In addition to water, some growers recommend using a product specially designed to aid in flushing, like Grotek's Final Flush. These types of products are formulated to remove excess fertilizer salts and are typically designed for hydroponic grows. Be sure to follow label instructions if you decide to use a flushing product.

HARVESTING

After you've timed your harvest and completed the flush (if you're using one), it's finally time to harvest your plants! There are two basic ways you can harvest your marijuana to protect the plants and maximize their cannabinoid content:

1 **Cut the entire plant down.** This is the standard method if you're growing indoors. Using sharp shears, simply cut the main stem near the growing medium.

2 **Cut individual branches.** If you have a large plant outside, you might harvest individual branches rather than attempting to

wrestle with a 10' monster marijuana plant loaded with heavy buds. When you cut the branches, try to choose branches that have a fork: This will make it easier to hang the branches in the manicuring stage.

To harvest like a pro, you'll also want to follow these simple tips:

- **Limit light exposure.** Harvest at the end of a dark photoperiod if you're growing indoors, and very early in the morning if you're growing outdoors. Limiting light exposure will minimize the amount of degradation your resin glands experience during harvest (light destroys cannabinoids). Some indoor growers will even leave their plants in complete darkness for a full 24 hours before harvesting.

- **Prepare your drying space ahead of time.** You'll want to move your plants into the drying space as quickly as possible so they can be hung. Don't attempt to store freshly harvested marijuana in an enclosed space for long before hanging it, as it will only increase the risk of bud rot. Once in the drying space, you can suspend whole plants upside down from monofilament fishing line, or you can hook branches over a line. If you're using a closet to dry your buds, you can use wire coat hangers to hang the freshly harvested plants.

- **Be careful when transporting freshly harvested plants.** If you have a lot of plants to transport, consider buying a canvas tarp you can gently wrap around the newly harvested plants. This will minimize the amount of crushing damage. You can also transport freshly harvested plants and branches in large plastic bins, but be careful not to pack them in.

- **Give yourself lots of time on harvest day.** Your harvest work doesn't end with cutting the plants down! Allow plenty of time for cutting, hanging, and manicuring.

- **Manicure along the way.** If you have just one or two plants, only harvest as much as you can manicure at once, and process buds as you go. It's perfectly acceptable to harvest a marijuana plant in stages, taking branches and buds over the course of a day or two while you're busy manicuring.

MANICURING

Manicuring is a vital step to producing high-quality, attractive marijuana buds. The beautiful, frosty green buds you see in pictures are the result of careful manicuring. During a manicure, you'll remove extra leaves and trim your buds down—much like giving them a haircut. (See Figure 8.2.) It can be a lengthy process, so when you're ready to manicure, it's a good idea to have all of your equipment ready beforehand and find a comfortable place where you can sit and work on your buds for a while.

Before jumping into the steps to manicuring your buds, however, keep in mind that there are different approaches to both manicuring and drying. There's no "right" or "wrong" way to do so—only the way that gives you the buds you want.

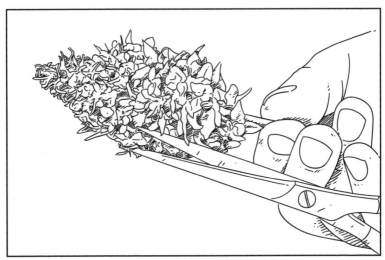

▲ Figure 8.2: Manicuring

At the most basic level, there are two types of manicuring:

1 **Wet manicure.** Here, you manicure your plants immediately after harvest, when the leaves are still full of moisture.

2 **Dry manicure.** Here, you manicure your plants after they've been hanging in the dry area for a few days, so the leaves are dry and brittle.

Many growers consider a dry manicure to be gentler on the buds, because the big fan leaves cloak the hanging plant in humidity, which slows the drying process. Others prefer a wet manicure because it's easier to remove more of the leaves around the bud and the resulting smoke when the bud is lit is more mellow.

For your first harvest, a wet manicure is a great place to start, but feel free to experiment! You can manicure some buds wet, let others dry for a day or two and then manicure, and fully dry the others. This is all part of the learning experience as you create your own signature marijuana.

When you are getting ready to manicure, you'll also need the following equipment:

- **Sharp trimming snippers.** Fiskars is a popular brand that makes very sharp, precise snippers.

- **Latex gloves.** These will protect your hands from sticky resin while manicuring.

- **Isopropyl alcohol.** To clean your scissors (and hands, if necessary) after use. Manicuring is sticky work!

- **Trays.** Baking sheets are great for catching trimmings as you work. On a tight hand-trim, you'll be removing sugar leaves that you definitely don't want to throw out!

WHAT ARE SUGAR LEAVES?

When you harvest your bud, you'll notice tiny leaves sticking out from the flowers. These leaves are often frosted with resin and are referred to as "sugar leaves." Whether or not you keep the sugar leaves on your manicured buds is a matter of personal preference. Some growers leave them on for drying, while others snip them close to the flower to expose more of the bud and produce a more mellow smoke when the bud is lit. Whatever you do, don't throw them out: Sugar leaves are quality trim you can use to make edibles.

As you're working, be prepared for a strong odor—even stronger than flowering plants. Make sure you're working in a space with good ventilation and odor control. This might mean trimming in your grow space.

Once you have all of your gear in place, follow these steps to produce a high-quality manicure:

1 If you're doing a wet manicure: As you harvest your plants, immediately remove all the large fan leaves and bigger secondary leaves. (You can even remove these a day before harvest to save time.) A good rule of thumb is if a leaf has a visible stem, snip it off. Try to cut these as close to the main stem as possible, or pinch them off with your fingers. These leaves should be composted: They don't contain any THC and have little value.

2 Cut the branches into workable sections and work with one branch at a time. Hold your branch by the stem, and try to handle the buds as little as possible while manicuring.

3 Working over a tray to catch the trim, start trimming away excess leaves and bits of stem from the buds on the branch. Rotate the buds as you're working to ensure an even trim. Don't cut into the flowers. A good general rule is to keep your snipper blades flat against the flower, rather than pointed into the flower itself. The main stem of the branch will remain intact in order to hang the buds after manicuring.

4 Keep trimming until you're satisfied with the look of your buds. Ideally, you'll want a nice, compact bud with no visible leaves sticking out.

5 When you're done, gently tap the branch with your snippers to shake out any leaf bits that remain in the buds. Depending

on how much you are manicuring, you might have to stop and clean resin from your trimmers if they're sticking.

6 Once you're done manicuring, you'll hang your buds by the branch to dry.

PRO TIP: SAVE THAT RESIN!

You may have heard growers who trim without gloves talk fondly about "finger hash." These are basically balls of resin that collect on your skin during manicuring. By rolling your resin-covered fingers together, you can separate the little balls and use them to get some potent smoke. You can also save the resin that builds on your tools and equipment—and even your latex gloves—during manicuring. Try putting your sticky latex gloves in the freezer to harden the resin, or just throw them in a cupboard and let them dry. You'll then be able to flake off the resin for use.

DRYING

Drying your buds is the next step after manicuring. Ideally, drying should be done in a dark, low-humidity (45–55 percent) environment with a temperature of 65°F–75°F. You want it dark because light degrades cannabinoids and will affect the potency of your marijuana. Low humidity will help prevent bud rot. Drying should also be a slow, controlled process: Don't use a fan pointed at your buds, or external heat, to hurry it along. This will result in harsh, unpleasant notes to your final product.

After you've completed the manicure, move your buds to the drying area to hang them on monofilament fishing life, clothes hangers, or any other support rack of your choosing. (See Figure 8.3.) Some growers use their grow space as a drying area to cut down on odor. However, if you've pressed your growing space into service again and have new plants growing in it, you'll need to find another drying area.

As your buds slowly dry, they will gradually lose moisture—but the point isn't to dry them until they're brittle: Dried buds will still retain moisture deep inside. This deeper moisture will come out during the curing stage, to result in a wonderfully sticky yet smooth smoke.

Exactly how long you should dry depends on your environment and your manicuring approach. If you chose a dry manicure and left the fan leaves on when you harvested, drying can take five to seven days, or even longer. If you've already removed the fan leaves and chose a wet manicure, smaller buds can dry in three to five days, while larger buds can take one week to dry. It really depends on your environment; hotter, dryer rooms will result in a faster dry, while cooler and more humid rooms will slow the process down.

While the buds are drying, check on them daily to make sure they are drying properly. Look for signs of bud rot, mold, or pests. Kill insects and mites with tape or your fingers and, if you're drying in your growing area, make sure you thoroughly treat the space for pests before you plant anything else. If you find mold growing on your buds, cut out the affected sections and throw them away, and consider moving your buds to an area with lower humidity.

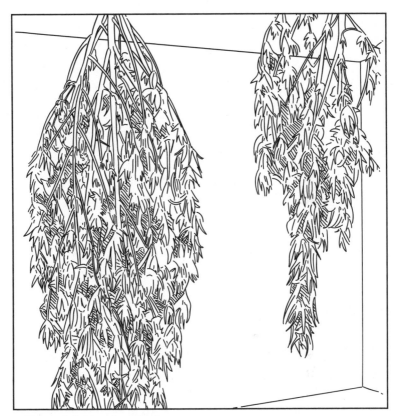

▲ Figure 8.3: Hanging Plants

Signs the buds are dry:

1 The larger stems are brittle enough to break with an audible snap, leaving no strings or plant material at the break.

2 When you gently squeeze a bud, it feels dry on the outside but still spongy in the middle.

USING A DRYING RACK OR BOX

Some growers hang their buds to dry for a few days, then snip the buds from the stems and transfer them to drying racks or drying boxes. Others remove most of the stem material at the manicure stage and complete the entire drying process on drying racks.

If you choose to use a drying rack or box, you will first spread the buds out on the rack or in the box. Don't stack the buds too deeply: This will crush valuable trichomes and reduce the quality. If you're drying on a rack, gently turn the buds every day. Turning them regularly will help prevent mold damage, ensure more even drying, and prevent the buds from flattening on one side.

While this is a perfectly viable method for drying, and commonly used by large-scale growers, it's recommended that as a beginning grower, you start off by hanging your buds to dry until they are ready to be cured. It's a gentler approach, and there's less risk of damaging your valuable buds.

PRO TIP: MAKE YOUR OWN DRYING BOX

While you can find drying boxes online, it's easy to make your own using window screens. Place one screen in a large wooden or cardboard box, first inserting small blocks of wood in the four corners of the box for the screen frame to rest on. Next, load the screen with a single layer of buds. Insert four more wood blocks at the corners of the screen, and stack a second screen in the box. Add another layer of buds. You can stack layers of bud right up the top 2" or so of the box. Remember to turn the buds daily to help prevent mold!

CURING

Curing your buds is the final step after drying—and it's one you definitely won't want to skip. Curing is similar to drying, but it's performed even more slowly, and always done in an airtight contained environment like a jar or box. During curing, the remaining moisture will be evenly distributed throughout the buds. Curing is essential for smooth, satisfying marijuana. The ideal curing container is a wide-mouthed glass Mason jar.

To cure your buds, snip the stems into sections (if you haven't already) and lightly pack the buds into a jar. Only put as many into the jar as will easily stack without additional pressure. When it's full, seal the jar and store it in dark, cool place. Repeat with remaining buds and jars.

The first day of curing is especially important. About 3 hours after you've packed and stored your curing jars, check to see if the insides of the jars have visible moisture on the sides. If they do, your buds weren't ready for curing. In this case, take the buds out of your curing jars and place them in a paper bag for another full day to finish the drying process. Crimp the top of the bag to slow moisture loss.

Once your buds are packed and curing, open the jars daily throughout the cure and gently move the buds around with your finger. This will help release any built-up humidity and prevent mold. A good curing jar is a protected microenvironment that will very gently complete the drying process.

In total, curing should take between two and six weeks, depending on the size of the buds, their moisture level, and the strain. Refer to online resources or your local seed bank for more information on how long you should cure your own grow, based on the strain you chose and the size and moisture of your buds. Once cured completely, you can enjoy your homegrown marijuana!

PRO TIP: ADD FRUIT

In some cases, your buds may dry out a little too fast during curing and you'll want to rehydrate them. (Bud that had been cured too fast may result in a harsh smoke.) The best way to rehydrate your bud is to add fresh buds to the curing jar. If you don't have fresh buds, you can also use fruit peels. Try adding a little lemon or orange peel to your curing jar and stirring it around with your buds. Don't overdo it: A 1" slice of peel should be plenty at first, and be sure to keep a close eye on your buds to make sure they aren't getting too much moisture and developing a fungus. Over time, the peel will release moisture back into the buds and also impart a delightful citrusy note.

STORING

Ideally, you want to store your cured buds in an airtight, lightproof environment. Although it's not uncommon to see bud shipped in vacuum-sealed plastic bags, it's best to avoid using vacuum-sealed plastic bags if possible, because the buds can be crushed during vacuum sealing. Instead, consider buying a vacuum sealer that works with glass jars fitted with special vacuum lids. There are many good, affordable brands on the market, so shop around. There are even custom-designed marijuana jars that are vacuum sealed and track the humidity inside the jar. Marijuana stored in vacuum-sealed glass jars will last for months, as there is little degradation of the THC. Once sealed, store your jars in the refrigerator.

If you don't have a vacuum-sealer, you can store your cured buds in a glass jar with a tight lid. In this case, your buds will lose potency faster than if they had been vacuum-sealed, but you'll still enjoy your harvest for many weeks.

When you take a new jar out and open it (if it's been vacuum-sealed) you should hear the slight hiss of releasing air, letting you know that the vacuum seal has been maintained and your buds are almost as fresh and potent as they were the day you finished curing.

PRO TIP: DON'T FREEZE YOUR BUD

You may have heard of freezing cured buds: This is one piece of advice you can safely ignore. In fact, freezing will turn the remaining moisture in the buds into ice crystals, which will damage the resin glands when the buds are defrosted.

FIVE TIPS TO REMEMBER

You've successfully grown your marijuana plants, and are ready to reap the rewards. Harvesting, curing, and manicuring your buds will be the final steps in the process—and they are steps you'll want to savor. Use the following main tips from this chapter to effectively harvest, cure, and manicure your marijuana:

1   **Make a schedule ahead of time.** Set aside plenty of time on harvest day so you can manicure your buds.

2   **Pick a manicuring method.** When harvesting, either cut the whole plant down to manicure at once, or cut the plant down in sections and manicure as you go. Using sharp snippers, manicure the buds by trimming as close as possible to the flower without cutting into the flower.

3   **Pick a good drying environment.** Hang your buds in a cool, low-humidity room. In a standard wet-manicure, drying should take about three to five days.

4   **Check in on curing buds frequently.** Remember to "turn" the buds in the jar daily to reduce the risk of bud rot.

5   **Store cured buds in an airtight container.** Ideally, you should use a vacuum-sealed glass jar. If you don't have a vacuum-sealer, you can store buds in regular glass jars that are tightly closed. Keeping your bud in the refrigerator will help it retain its potency for longer.

CHAPTER 9

Pests

No matter how clean you keep your grow area, or how carefully you select your strains, at some point while growing marijuana, you may have to deal with pests. Outdoors, predators both large and very small will want to feast on your plants. Indoors, your plants may be attacked by sucking, chewing, and burrowing insects that can multiply with astonishing speed, threatening to destroy your whole grow area. Fortunately, there are easy ways to handle pest infestations during your grow—and even prevent them from occurring.

In this chapter, you'll explore the most common marijuana pests and ways to both prevent them from attacking your plants and remove them should they manage to invade your grow site. While this chapter deals exclusively with predatory insects and mites, you will find information on how to deal with larger outdoor pests such as deer and rabbits in Chapter 5, and information on how to deal with fungal problems in Chapter 7.

THE PEST CONTROL HIERARCHY

Before jumping into the details of common pests you may encounter during your marijuana grow, it is important to note that there is a recommended order of operations you should follow when it comes to pests and your plants:

1 **Prevention.** The best defense is a good offense. By taking steps early in your planning stages, and sticking with it throughout your grow, you can help prevent a lot of pest problems. These early steps include planning for maximum protection and keeping your grow area clean.

2 **Manual control.** If you see a caterpillar on your plant, pick it off! The same goes for beetles, aphids, and other insects you'll discover in the following sections of this chapter. You can gently pick off many pests or even wipe them away with a paper towel or rag (making sure to never touch any other plants and immediately remove the rag from your growing area). Refer to the section on control later in this chapter for more information on methods of manual control for each common pest you may encounter.

3 **Organic control.** This includes the use of any control/eradication solutions that are all natural, such as horticultural oil. Refer to the section on control later in this chapter for more information on methods of organic control for each common pest you may encounter.

4 **Chemical control.** This should only be done as a last resort, and only then to stop an invasion before it wipes out your entire crop. Even under those circumstances, it's still recommended

that you removing infected plants first. Never use anything on a marijuana plant you wouldn't want to put in your body. Refer to the section on control later in this chapter for more information on methods of chemical control.

COMMON PESTS

The first step to pest prevention and control is understanding the common pests that target marijuana plants. After all, from planning your grow to preparing for harvest, you'll want to know the threats you may face. Some pests are obvious on sight, while others will be noticeable from tiny telltale signs on the marijuana plant. The following sections outline the most common pests that may set their sights on your marijuana garden.

SPIDER MITES

Spider mites are one of the most feared pests in marijuana gardening. These tiny, eight-legged arachnids are barely visible to the naked eye but can easily destroy your plants in a matter of days. These miniature destroyers attach to the underside of marijuana leaves and suck out the plant juices. (See Figure 9.1.)

As their population increases, they spin webs across the leaves of the plant; these webs are visible by spraying the leaves with water, causing the webs to shine. (See Figure 9.2.)

The first visible signs of spider mite damage are typically small, yellowish blotches on the tops of leaves. These spots can quickly multiply as the mites' population increases. Over time, the leaves will curl and begin dropping.

▲ Figure 9.1: Spider Mite

▲ Figure 9.2: Infested Plant

APHIDS

Aphids are tiny, soft-bodied sucking insects that attach to your plants' stems and tissues and suck out sap and juice. They also encourage the growth of sooty mold, which thrives on aphids' honeydew. Aphids are extremely common both indoors and outdoors, and they can sometimes be spread by ants, who "farm" aphids so they can extract their sweet honeydew.

Aphids are considerably larger than mites and should be easily visible to the naked eye. They also multiply with speed and will quickly form clusters or colonies on new plant growth.

CATERPILLARS

Caterpillars are the larvae of winged insects like butterflies and moths. These pests tend to be a bigger problem for outdoor gardens, where butterflies and moths have easy access to your plants to lay eggs.

Caterpillars are generally not difficult to spot. Although there are many different types of caterpillars, they are all larger than other sucking or chewing insects. They are voracious feeders and can reduce a plant to a bare stem in just a few days. To identify a caterpillar infestation, look for leaves that are chewed from the leaf margin toward the center. You can also spot caterpillars by their droppings: Small black spots on your leaves that look like black pepper might be a sign of a caterpillar infestation.

LEAF MINERS

Leaf miners are tiny fly larvae that burrow under the "skin" of your marijuana leaves. They leave looping, telltale scars on the leaves.

These scars are largely cosmetic and mostly affect outdoor plants, so you may choose to simply leave them alone. If the infestation becomes serious, however, it may impact your plants' growth.

MEALYBUGS

Mealybugs are soft-bodied, sap-sucking insects that form clusters of adults covered with white, waxy fluff. They are a particular nuisance for indoor growers (outside, mealybugs are often contained by natural predators).

Mealybug damage causes leaves to turn yellow and drop, while also stunting the plant's growth and hastening the spread of sooty mold. These insects particularly target new plant growth.

SCALE INSECTS

Scale insects are small sucking insects covered with a hard shell. They appear like small dots or scabs on the plant's surface. The actual insect is under the protective covering. Scale insects tend to be a bigger problem for indoor growers, but infestations are often fairly easy to manage and don't cause rapid decline of your marijuana.

WHITEFLY

Whiteflies are tiny flies that lay eggs on your plants. Both adults and larvae suck juices from your plants, resulting in damage that resembles mite damage. As with scale insects, whitefly damage is rarely fatal, but they will cause your plants to slow in growth and can reduce the harvest. Whiteflies also produce sweet honeydew that encourages the growth of black sooty mold.

Whiteflies are easy to distinguish from mites with a simple test: Shake your leaves and look for a cloud of tiny whiteflies to emerge from the leaves.

PEST PREVENTION

It's worth saying again: the best defense is a good offense. With proper planning and management, you can avoid a lot of pest problems from the start. The following sections outline simple ways you can help prevent pests from attacking your outdoor or indoor grow.

⇒ WHAT ARE THE BEST STRAINS FOR PEST PREVENTION?

When you're researching strains, try to pick one(s) with your growing environment in mind. Short, squat *indicas* tend to be more susceptible to fungi and pests, while *sativas* have greater fungus resistance and rely on their rapid growth to outrun pest problems. Therefore, a *sativa* may be better suited for an outdoor growing environment, where there are more pests.

OUTDOOR PREVENTION

Outdoor growers have a natural ally in Mother Nature. Although it's true there are unlimited pests outdoors, there are also natural predators and beneficial insects that will help keep pest populations in control. You can bolster this natural protection by not creating a large plot containing only tempting marijuana plants. Instead, mix other companion plants among your marijuana if possible. Some of the best companion plants for marijuana include:

- **Corn.** Savvy farmers know that corn and marijuana do well together. Not only is corn a great camouflaging crop, but also it lures pests away from your marijuana.

- **Marigold.** These delightful flowers are one of the most popular companion plants to marijuana. They are said to increase the growth rate of nearby plants, while simultaneously deterring beetles and other chewing insects, including whiteflies.

- **Sunflower.** Sunflowers are powerful attractants (a term used to describe a companion plant that draws nasty pests away from your main plants—in this case marijuana). Sunflowers attract bugs that eat the dreaded spider mite, as well as gnats and scale insects.

Various herbs are also beneficial to plant near marijuana, although it can be more difficult to keep herbs thriving unless you have constant access to your garden. If you *are* growing in your backyard, or a greenhouse where you have constant access, consider adding herbs like basil, cilantro, peppermint, garlic, and dill to your garden. These herbs repel a variety of insects— including mites, aphids, beetles, and caterpillars—and they are also delicious.

INDOOR PREVENTION

As an indoor gardener, you won't have the advantage of natural predators, but you will benefit from a totally controlled grow space. The key to preventing pest problems indoors is to practice excellent hygiene, which will also help reduce the risk of fungi. Follow these simple tips to reduce the risk of your grow area becoming infested with pests:

1 **Never use your outdoor tools or equipment indoors.** Once you've used a tool or piece of equipment outside, it should never be taken into your grow room without being thoroughly sanitized. The quickest way to get pests in your grow space is to invite them in on dirty tools.

2 **Keep your grow room clean.** This means keeping the floor swept and dry, and never leaving old organic material like used potting soil lying around. Your grow room doesn't have to look like a surgical suite at a hospital, but it should be clean and tidy. Pests thrive in damp, dark corners where they can hide.

3 **Change your clothes before entering your grow room.** If you've been outside, don't go straight into your indoor grow area. Change into a clean pair of pants and shirt.

4 **Wash your hands.** Again, you're not scrubbing in for surgery, but you should wash your hands every time you head into your grow space to handle your plants.

5 **Don't reuse potting soil or growing medium.** This can be tempting because it saves money, but it's a bad idea. Over time, your exhausted potting soil will be more likely to harbor insect eggs. Instead, incorporate your old growing medium into your outdoor garden: Your outdoor vegetables will love it.

6 **Keep your plants healthy.** Marijuana is a naturally vigorous plant that will easily outgrow many pests. By contrast, weak, sick plants invite attacks from pests and diseases. Focus on growing healthy marijuana, and you'll have fewer pest problems.

7 Pay close attention. You should be inspecting your plants regularly, looking for signs of problems. Flip the leaves upside down and look closely for insects, eggs, or webs. Check the stems and leaf nodes as well. By spotting stray insects and dealing with them quickly, you can prevent a huge problem later.

PEST CONTROL

In the event that a pest problem does occur, you'll need to eradicate it. It can be tempting to reach for a pesticide first, but in fact that should often be your last resort. In general, you always want to start with the least toxic option (manual control, such as picking a caterpillar off the plant and relocating it away from your grow site) and gradually use stronger organic methods only as necessary. You'll find that, by paying close attention and acting quickly, you can stop many problems without the use of a single product, whether you're growing indoors or outdoors.

The following are the best ways of dealing with the different common marijuana pests:

- **Spider mites.** Eradicate small spider mite infestations by manually removing infested leaves and wiping away colonies with your gloved fingers or a sponge. (With all pest control, never let an infested sponge or glove touch other plants). If that doesn't work, try an organic option like garlic spray. If this fails, graduate to stronger solutions like neem oil, horticultural oil, or pyrethrum. Spider mites have a natural reproductive cycle of about five days, meaning that you need to re-treat infected plants every five days until the infestation is gone. If you can't control the infestation, remove or destroy the plant. If your plant is close to harvest, you can harvest it immediately, but be aware that spider mites also love buds, so to prevent the spread of mites, don't hang a potentially infested bud with other buds.

- **Aphids.** Eradicate aphids by manually removing them with your gloved fingers—or a napkin or rag. They are easy to remove by simply wiping them away. Make sure to look under the leaves as well so you can remove any aphids hiding there. Outdoors, you can spray your marijuana with a hose to literally blast away the aphids. If manual removal doesn't work, or there are too many to remove by hand, try horticultural soap or oil during vegetative growth. Pyrethrum is also a very effective aphid killer. Spot-treat small infestations. Aphids have a life cycle of about forty days, but they reproduce extremely quickly, so you'll need to treat your plants every week or so until the infestation is under control. If you're using a chemical control, don't spray your plants near harvest time.

- **Caterpillars.** To eradicate caterpillars, simply pick them off the plants. You can also use *Bacillus thuringiensis* (Bt), a naturally occurring bacteria that kills caterpillars. Bt is available as a bait or a powder. In addition, pyrethrum will kill mature caterpillars. If you're using a chemical control, don't spray your plants near harvest time.

- **Leaf miners.** Treating a leaf miner infestation can be difficult because the larvae are naturally protected inside the leaf. Try cutting off and discarding affected leaves. You can use sticky traps to catch mature adults and keep the population under control. Neem oil used as a soil drench can also help, as the plant will take the neem up through its roots and into its vascular system, killing any leaf miners that are feasting on the plant. Neem is a gentle pesticide, but you shouldn't use it on your plants near harvest time.

- **Mealybugs.** To eradicate mealybugs, physically remove them with your gloved hands or a cloth. You can also spray the plants with water to literally blast the bugs off your foliage. If that doesn't work, a solution of rubbing alcohol or insecticidal soap applied during vegetative growth can eliminate them. If you need a stronger solution, neem oil and pyrethrum are good options.

- **Scale insects.** If you see scale, first try simply scraping them off of your plant with your finger, then disposing of them and washing your hands before you handle your plants again. You can also use a cotton swab dipped in rubbing alcohol to wipe the bugs away. Scale insects don't reproduce as quickly as some other pests, but you may still have to re-treat every few weeks. If physical removal doesn't work, you can use neem oil, horticultural oil, or insecticidal soap during vegetative growing, or pyrethrum. Don't use these solutions close to harvest time.

- **Whiteflies.** Eradicate whiteflies with a pyrethrum spray or garlic spray. They have a relatively fast life cycle in warmer environments, so treat weekly until you don't see any more signs of infestation.

PRO TIP: AVOID INSECTICIDAL SOAP DURING FLOWERING

Insecticidal soaps are a favorite tool of the organic gardener—but they're not recommended for use in your marijuana garden during flowering. Insecticidal soaps are heavier than regular sprays, so they are known to knock precious trichomes off your flowering plants. Overall, it's never a good idea to spray a flowering marijuana plant, but if you must, try to avoid using insecticidal soap and instead use another solution like neem.

COMMON PESTICIDES

In general, pesticides should be your last option for pest control. Good gardening practices like keeping your grow site clean and not cross-using indoor and outdoor tools can really help reduce the risk of pest problems. If you *do* need to reach for a pesticide, however, it's recommended that you use one of the organic options in the following sections. You can use these with any grow, indoors or outdoors, but always follow label directions and use the appropriate safety gear when called for. As with all chemicals, don't use them near harvest time. If you're dealing with plants that are experiencing serious infestations near harvest, it's better to cut away the infested parts and harvest early, making sure to isolate those buds as they dry to prevent the spread of pests.

Bacillus Thuringiensis

B. thuringiensis (Bt) is one of the most common microbial pest control options used in organic gardens. Bt is a beneficial bacteria that is toxic to chewing caterpillars. It's available as a powder, liquid, dust, and granule. While it is nontoxic to people, it's recommended that you only use Bt if you have a caterpillar infestation—not as a preventive measure.

Garlic Spray

Garlic spray is a time-tested organic pesticide and pest deterrent. And thanks to garlic's natural antibiotic and fungicidal properties, this spray can also protect against fungal and bacterial infections. To make your own garlic oil spray, soak 3 ounces of peeled, minced garlic in 2 ounces of mineral oil overnight. Then, strain the mixture, and combine with 2 cups of water in a large spray bottle. You can also add a liquid dish soap (unscented and without any additives; Mrs. Meyer's is a great option) to help the spray spread and stick. Add 2 tablespoons of dish soap for every 1 gallon of spray. This solution should only be used on plants in vegetative growth.

Horticultural Oil

Horticultural oil is typically made from mineral oil. This product works by forming an oily covering over the insect, which drowns or suffocates them. The key to using it effectively is to get good coverage of your plants and reapply as often as needed. You may have to reapply weekly, or every few days, depending on the results you're getting, and avoid spraying oil on flowering plants.

Neem Oil

Neem is an astonishingly effective organic garden aid for the marijuana grower. It's a pesticide, insect repellent, and fungicide wrapped up in one. Neem is also both a topical treatment and a systemic treatment that you can mix with your regular water and feed to your plants through the growing medium. As a topical spray, neem oil is effective against spider mites, aphids, mealybugs, beetles, and more. You can also use neem as a weekly preventive spray throughout the stages of your plant's growth.

⚜ WHAT IS SO SPECIAL ABOUT NEEM?

Neem oil is derived from the neem tree (*Azadirachta indica*), which is native to India. Neem oil isn't only used to help kill pests and prevent fungi: It's also used in alternative medicine to treat parasites, upset stomach, diabetes, and even gum disease. Neem is approved for use in organic gardens and is considered nontoxic to humans when used as directed for gardening use in regular quantities. If there's one organic pest control product you should keep around, neem oil is it.

Pyrethrum

Pyrethrum is the strongest pesticide recommended for use in marijuana growing, but when you do use it, it can save your entire crop. This product is made from the dried flower heads of the *Chrysanthemum cinerariifolium* daisy. It's also available as an extract sold under the name "pyrethrin." A synthetic version of this product called "pyrethroid" is also available, but it should never be used on your marijuana under any circumstances, as it's much stronger than pyrethrum. Pyrethrum kills a wide variety of insects and mites on contact, including aphids, spider mites, beetles, thrips, and whiteflies. Follow the label directions and don't apply to flowering plants or in the three weeks before harvesting.

PRO TIP: SPRAY SAFELY

When you're working with chemicals, always take safety precautions—such as wearing gloves, safety glasses, and a mouth cover to avoid inhaling sprays—and follow label directions. You can buy gloves in your local garden center, as well as basic respirators. Wear long shirts and pants and closed-in shoes, and take the necessary precautions depending on indoor or outdoor use. Do the proper research so you are fully informed on the best methods, appropriate solutions, and safe period for insect control. You should also treat a smaller "test" area of plants first, to see how they react to the treatment. When you are ready to spray, do it early in the light cycle, and be careful of your lights and electrical equipment. Raise your lights if necessary. Finally, never mix multiple products into the same spray unless it's indicated on the label, and always empty and clean your equipment after use. It's not a good idea to store mixed sprays in an unmarked container, because you can easily forget what's in the bottle.

SAVING A TROUBLED GROW

It's not possible to list every possible ailment that might afflict your marijuana plants. In addition to the fungus and pest problems outlined previously, marijuana can also be vulnerable to various wilts, blights, and various types of mildew, mold, and even algae. Remember: You're creating a perfect grow environment, so it's inevitable that some other plants and insects will agree that it's a wonderful place to live. You can find more information online, or through a seed bank, on other pests and fungi, light and watering issues, etc. Revisit previous chapters in this book for information on larger pests, as well as correcting fertilizer, lighting, and other problems.

Above all else, pay close attention to your plants and inspect them often. There's no substitute for catching a developing problem early. Look for telltale signs, like leaves turning yellow or curling, black or brown spots, deformed leaves, or the presence of droppings or webs.

FIVE TIPS TO REMEMBER

When you first start out growing marijuana, it can be very intimidating, especially if you don't have much experience in gardening in general. Fortunately, the information in this book is here to help you evolve from a beginner (who might have never raised so much as a houseplant before) to an experienced marijuana grower. And among the details, there is a simple truth: At the end of the day, marijuana is a hardy plant that has thrived alongside humans for thousands of years. While things might not go exactly as planned during your first grow, don't give up! Keep at it, revisit the different chapters in this book, and remember these five key things:

1 **The first step in pest control is prevention.** Taking steps to make your plants less vulnerable to pests early in your garden or grow room design can save a lot of trouble later on.

2 Pay close attention to your plants. If you see brown spots on your leaves, or tiny webs, or droppings, take rapid action to isolate the problem before it spreads.

3 Always start with the least toxic option. In most cases, this will be some type of manual control, whether that's picking off caterpillars or using a strong jet of water to blast away insects.

4 Start gently. If you have to use a treatment product, start with the mildest option, like a garlic spray, before reaching for a chemical. Always follow label instructions and wear appropriate safety gear when handling chemicals.

5 An early harvest is better than a spoiled crop. If your pest problem can't be controlled, don't hesitate to isolate and destroy infested plants. If it's near harvest, you can harvest these plants early and attempt to salvage some of the bud.

Resources

WEBSITES

General Hydroponics
https://generalhydroponics.com

High Times
https://hightimes.com

Leafly
www.leafly.com

Overgrow
https://overgrow.com

Rollitup
www.rollitup.org

Royal Queen Seeds
www.royalqueenseeds.com

SeedFinder
https://en.seedfinder.eu

Space Buckets
www.spacebuckets.com

Wikileaf
www.wikileaf.com

BOOKS

Bradley, Fern Marshall, Barbara W. Ellis, and Deborah L.
Martin (eds.). *The Organic Gardener's Handbook of Natural
Pest and Disease Control: A Complete Guide to Maintaining
a Healthy Garden and Yard the Earth-Friendly Way.* New
York: Rodale, 2010.

Cervantes, Jorge. *Marijuana Horticulture: The Indoor/Outdoor
Medical Grower's Bible.* Vancouver, WA: Van Patten
Publishing, 2006.

Green, Greg. *The Cannabis Breeder's Bible: The Definitive
Guide to Marijuana Genetics, Cannabis Botany and
Creating Strains for the Seed Market.* San Francisco: Green
Candy Press, 2005.

Green, Greg. *The Cannabis Grow Bible: The Definitive Guide
to Growing Marijuana for Recreational and Medical Use.*
San Francisco: Green Candy Press, 2017.

Rosenthal, Ed. *Marijuana Grower's Handbook: Your Complete
Guide for Medical and Personal Marijuana Cultivation.*
Oakland, CA: Quick American Publishing, 2010.

Glossary

AEROPONICS
Growing plants without a growing medium, instead providing water and nutrients through mist or spraying roots directly.

ASEXUAL REPRODUCTION
The process of producing plants from clones.

AUTOFLOWERING
Strains of marijuana that have been bred to flower after a certain number of weeks, no matter what the photoperiod is. These are good strains for short growing seasons.

BLOOM BOOSTER
A fertilizer with a higher phosphorus level.

BUCKETEER
A grower who uses the space bucket method.

BUD
A slang term for a marijuana flower.

CALYX
A very early flowering structure that forms at the plant's nodes. When they first emerge, they may be very small and impossible to see with the naked eye. Over time, the calyxes will grow and become recognizable as male or female preflowers.

CANNABIDIOL (CBD)
A cannabinoid found in marijuana that can sometimes be used medicinally.

CANNABINOID RECEPTORS
(Also called "CB1" and "CB2" receptors.) Specialized sites on cells in the human body where cannabinoids, including CBD and THC, can attach to the cells and exert their effects.

CANNABINOIDS
Chemicals produced both in the human body and by the marijuana plant. They are bioactive in the human body.

CANNABIS INDICA
(Also referred to as *indica*.) A subspecies of marijuana that is commonly grown indoors.

CANNABIS RUDERALIS
(Also referred to as *ruderalis*.) A subspecies of marijuana that is often used in breeding.

CANNABIS SATIVA
(Also referred to as C. *sativa*.) A species of marijuana commonly grown for consumption. *C. sativa* includes the subspecies *C. indica* and *C. ruderalis*. Plants with a dominant *C. sativa* phenome are sometimes referred to simply as *sativa* and are commonly grown outdoors.

CLONE
An exact genetic replica of an original plant.

COLA
A single large marijuana flower.

COTYLEDON LEAVES
The first immature leaves produced by a plant grown from seed; they do not have the mature leaf shape of the adult plant.

CURING
After the marijuana drying stage, the process of packing buds in an airtight contained environment, like a jar, and slowly reducing and evenly distributing the remaining moisture.

DAMPING OFF
A diseased condition of seedlings marked by the growth of *Pythium*.

DEEP WATER CULTURE (DWC)
A type of hydroponic growing system in which the plants are grown over reservoirs of water and nutrients.

DIOECIOUS
When male and female flowers are borne on separate, individual plants.

DRIP IRRIGATION SYSTEM
A type of microirrigation system in which plants are watered and fed through very small tubes that are often connected to a timer and release controlled amounts of water and fertilizer.

DRYING
The process of hanging freshly harvested marijuana plants long enough for most of the moisture to evaporate from the flowers and leaves.

EBB AND FLOW SYSTEM
A type of hydroponic growing system in which plants are grown on a table that is flooded with water and nutrients according to a specific schedule.

ELECTRICAL CONDUCTIVITY (EC)
A measure of the concentration of fertilizer salts in a hydroponic solution. EC is commonly used to measure the strength of fertilizers in hydroponic gardening.

ENDOCANNABINOIDS
Cannabinoids produced by the human body.

FLOWERING
The stage following vegetative growth and preflowering when a plant produces flowers.

FLUSHING
The practice of running large amounts of fresh water through a growing system before plants are harvested, in order to remove excess salt buildup and any remaining nutrients.

GERMINATING
Providing a seed with the right conditions to begin growing.

GIRDLING
When the string or wire encircling a plant stem cuts into the stem and risks strangling the plant.

GROW CABINET
A type of growing system, usually consisting of a hard-bodied structure like a dresser that has been modified with grow lights, ventilation, and other equipment.

GROW TENT
A tent that's been specially designed for horticultural purposes.

GUERRILLA GROWING
Using either public land or someone else's land to grow crops.

HARDENING OFF
The process of gradually acclimating an indoor plant to outdoor growing conditions.

HARVESTING
The process of cutting down adult plants for use.

HASH
Compressed resin from a flowering marijuana plant.

HEMP
A strain of marijuana, specifically *Cannabis sativa*, that has been bred to have negligible quantities of THC.

HERMAPHRODITE
A single plant that contains both male and female flowers.

HIGH INTENSITY DISCHARGE (HID) LIGHTS
Lights that produce a greater range of light wavelengths than standard incandescent or florescent bulbs. They are often used in indoor marijuana gardening.

HYBRID
Offspring resulting from crossbreeding two different gene pools.

HYDROPONICS
A soilless growing method that uses nutrients in a water solution to grow plants.

LANDRACE STRAINS
Unique strains of marijuana that have evolved in a natural environment and have never been crossed with another strain.

LIGHT CYCLE
The alternating periods of light and darkness in a 24-hour period.

LOW-STRESS TRAINING (LST)
A method of training marijuana plants to grow in desired directions that relies on bending and shaping the young branches.

MANICURING
The act of trimming freshly harvested marijuana buds to remove extra leaves and other unwanted parts before drying and curing (wet manicure).

NODE
Where the stem meets the branch.

NPK RATIO
A standard formulation used in fertilizers to indicate how much of the three primary nutrients (nitrogen, phosphorus, potassium) a particular fertilizer product has, as measured by weight.

NUTRIENT FILM TECHNIQUE (NFT)
A hydroponic gardening method in which marijuana plants are grown in wide tubes or gutters that are placed on an angle, allowing a thin, continuous stream of water and nutrients to nourish the plants.

PHOTOPERIOD
The ratio of light to dark in a 24-hour period.

PHYTOCANNABINOIDS
Cannabinoids produced by the marijuana plant.

PHYTOCHEMICALS
Chemicals produced by plants that may have beneficial effects in humans.

PISTIL
The sex organ of a female plant.

PREFLOWERING
The stage of a marijuana's plant life cycle just before flowering, when the plant reveals its sex.

PRUNING
The act of removing select branches to achieve a desired effect, such as shaping a plant to a particular growing space.

ROOT BOUND
When a plant's roots have filled its growing container.

SCREEN OF GREEN (SCROG)
A method of training marijuana plants to grow horizontally along a screen suspended over a growing area.

SEA OF GREEN (SOG)
A high-density method of growing marijuana plants that allows growers to pack many plants into a tight space by focusing on the top bud only and triggering flowering as early as possible.

SEED BANK
A company that sells marijuana seeds.

SEEDLING STAGE
The stage of a marijuana plant's life cycle that occurs right after germination, during which young plants are beginning to produce mature leaves.

SEXING
The act of identifying whether a plant is male or female.

SINSEMILLA
From the Spanish word meaning "without seed," sinsemilla is an unpollinated female marijuana plant.

SPACE BUCKET
A bucket that has been turned into a self-contained growing environment, complete with ventilation, lights, and room enough for one plant.

STIPULE
A tiny hairlike structure that emerges from the node, near the calyx.

STRAIN
A type of marijuana that has been bred from select parents to encourage desired traits and effects.

STRETCHING
When the stem elongates during the flowering stage.

SUGAR LEAVES
Small leaves that emerge from marijuana flowers and are often coated with resin.

TAILING
When tiny white sprouts emerge from seeds at the end of the germination stage.

TAPROOT
The main root of a plant; grows vertically downward.

TETRAHYDROCANNABINOL (THC)
The psychoactive chemical in marijuana.

THINNING
The act of removing individual plants from a growing area, often to provide the remaining plants with more growing space.

TOPPING
A type of pruning that is performed only on the top node of the plant to encourage branching of the main stem.

TOTAL DISSOLVED SOLIDS (TDS)
A measure (in parts-per-million) of how much of certain substances are found in water; commonly used in hydroponic gardening to measure how strong a nutrient solution is.

TRANSPLANTING
The process of transferring a plant to a larger container or into the ground.

TRICHOME
The resin gland where THC and other cannabinoids are produced in a marijuana plant.

VEGETATIVE GROWTH
The stage of a marijuana's life cycle in which the plant is putting out mature leaves, forming a woody stem, and growing taller.

US/Metric
Conversion Chart

VOLUME CONVERSIONS	
US VOLUME MEASURE	**METRIC EQUIVALENT**
⅛ teaspoon	0.5 milliliter
¼ teaspoon	1 milliliter
½ teaspoon	2 milliliters
1 teaspoon	5 milliliters
½ tablespoon	7 milliliters
1 tablespoon (3 teaspoons)	15 milliliters
2 tablespoons (1 fluid ounce)	30 milliliters
¼ cup (4 tablespoons)	60 milliliters
⅓ cup	90 milliliters
½ cup (4 fluid ounces)	125 milliliters
⅔ cup	160 milliliters
¾ cup (6 fluid ounces)	180 milliliters
1 cup (16 tablespoons)	250 milliliters
1 pint (2 cups)	500 milliliters
1 quart (4 cups)	1 liter (about)

WEIGHT CONVERSIONS

US WEIGHT MEASURE	METRIC EQUIVALENT
½ ounce	15 grams
1 ounce	30 grams
2 ounces	60 grams
3 ounces	85 grams
¼ pound (4 ounces)	115 grams
½ pound (8 ounces)	225 grams
¾ pound (12 ounces)	340 grams
1 pound (16 ounces)	454 grams

OVEN TEMPERATURE CONVERSIONS

DEGREES FAHRENHEIT	DEGREES CELSIUS
200 degrees F	95 degrees C
250 degrees F	120 degrees C
275 degrees F	135 degrees C
300 degrees F	150 degrees C
325 degrees F	160 degrees C
350 degrees F	180 degrees C
375 degrees F	190 degrees C
400 degrees F	205 degrees C
425 degrees F	220 degrees C
450 degrees F	230 degrees C

BAKING PAN SIZES	
AMERICAN	**METRIC**
8 × 1½ inch round baking pan	20 × 4 cm cake tin
9 × 1½ inch round baking pan	23 × 3.5 cm cake tin
11 × 7 × 1½ inch baking pan	28 × 18 × 4 cm baking tin
13 × 9 × 2 inch baking pan	30 × 20 × 5 cm baking tin
2 quart rectangular baking dish	30 × 20 × 3 cm baking tin
15 × 10 × 2 inch baking pan	30 × 25 × 2 cm baking tin (Swiss roll tin)
9 inch pie plate	22 × 4 or 23 × 4 cm pie plate
7 or 8 inch springform pan	18 or 20 cm springform or loose bottom cake tin
9 × 5 × 3 inch loaf pan	23 × 13 × 7 cm or 2 lb narrow loaf or pâté tin
1½ quart casserole	1.5 liter casserole
2 quart casserole	2 liter casserole

Index

About the Author

MURPH WOLFSON is a master gardener with more than a decade of experience in writing and teaching gardening. He has been growing marijuana since he was thirteen—although his grows are much more successful today.